How
WRITE
FORMAT
PUBLISH
PROMOTE

your book without

spending

ANY MONEY

A
CREATIVINDIE
GUIDE BY

DEREK
MURPHY

Hope you like this book!

If you need help with anything, feel free to get in touch.
A short review on Amazon would be hugely appreciated.

Sincerely, Derek Murphy

Twitter: @creativindie | Facebook.com/creativindie

WRITE, FORMAT, PUBLISH, PROMOTE
Copyright © 2014 by DEREK MURPHY

Cover design by Derek Murphy,
Formatting by Jake Muelle

ISBN: 978-0-9846551-3-7
First Edition: May 2014

10 9 8 7 6 5 4 3 2 1

creativINDIE

"For books are not absolutely dead things, but do contain a potency of life in them to be as active as that soul was whose progeny they are; nay, they do preserve as in a vial the purest efficacy and extraction of that living intellect that bred them."

—John Milton, Areopagitica

"This is the cusp of an age at least as exciting and as brimful of potential as the early days of the printing press." —Sara Sheridan

"

"Only a few short years ago, the average stay-at-home mom spent her relaxation time reading Jackie Collins and staring at the pool boy. Now, half of them are outselling Jackie Collins writing porn about the pool boy."

—Pete Morin, Surviving in the Amazon Jungle

WELCOME

So you want to publish a book, eh? That's great! There's never been a better time. The Internet and the rise of social media have made publishing a book, growing your audience and becoming a successful author a possibility for anybody. Getting an agent or publishing through a mainstream company is no longer required (and in some cases, disadvantageous). You really can self-publish, connect with readers, inspire hundreds of thousands of downloads and make a lot of money. But it isn't easy.

For a first time author, writing and publishing a book can be a daunting prospect. There's so much to learn: how to finish writing the book and get it ready for publication; how to format it for print and ebook; how and where to publish the book and distribute it to online and offline bookstores; how to get your book noticed amidst hundreds of thousands of others. For many authors, the entire process of writing and publishing is such a steep learning curve, with so many confusing variables, that it can lead to frustration and stagnation, which is sometimes overcome by throwing money at whoever promises to do everything for you.

Unfortunately, many author publishing services and small presses know how to manage the publishing process, but don't have the talent or skill required to make your book look good and ultimately find success. Therefore, DIY publishing is not just about saving money; it's also about making sure you end up with a well-designed product that sells. However, if you don't have much experience with book design, marketing or sales, making the right design choices can be difficult.

I hope this book will help with that, and inspire you to make smarter publishing choices, no matter your budget.

Does the world really need another guide to publishing and formatting? There are dozens of books like this popping up, how is mine different? For starters, I think most guides are written by authors who have learned these skills to publish their own books. While they may be valuable, a lot are saying the same things; and although they know how to publish (the mechanics) they aren't really versed on the art (the aesthetics). As a book designer who's helped publish over 1000 books, I focus my attention on making products that sell. It's not enough to just put your book out there. If you want it to be successful, it has to look and feel professional, powerful, and captivating. It needs an air of authority. It has to be a thing of beauty.

To that end, I've spent the past several months building free tools and resources that will help you take more control over your publishing and create a beautiful book. This should make the DIY publishing journey much easier, should you choose to brave it. What follows is a guide to using those resources, which as an added bonus, should drastically reduce publishing, formatting and marketing costs.

This book contains a lot of references to online material—the epub and PDF versions have hyperlinks, but it's more difficult to direct you to the right place in the print version. If you visit my website you can download a PDF or Ebook version that you can read on your computer, so it will be easier to click the links:

www.creativindie.com/WFPP.pdf

WHAT THIS BOOK ISN'T ABOUT

There are other books that are more in-depth about writing and publishing, and much longer. However, many of them seem padded with personal biography and plugs for the author's books and services. Others are heavy on inspiration and motivation, which may leave you pumped up about writing, but in no way ensure that energy translates into publishing success. I've been told my writing is pessimistic; I prefer to call it pragmatic. In my experience, optimistic, positively charged authors are not necessarily better writers, nor more successful authors. Too much empty enthusiasm can even be demotivating, if not supported by the right skills and a lot of elbow grease.

Because I don't base my books on a prerequisite word count (a pre-planned decision to make a book a certain length) this book contains no padding or fluff. I get straight to the point. This is a practical guide meant to traverse specific publishing related barriers with targeted solutions. That way it'll be easily referenced and utilized; so you can spend less time reading and more time writing books. That said, the purpose of this book is mainly to introduce you to some free tools I've made to assist you in DIY publishing. Parts of it are very technical and possibly a little boring. If you aren't happy with it, please ask for a refund.

CAN I REALLY DO IT FOR FREE?

Yes, you can format, publish and market your book without spending any money, if you have a lot of time on your hands and want to learn some new skills. And I'm going to be giving you a lot of free resources to help you do just that. But personally, even though I can do all this stuff myself, I choose to pay someone else to do the things I don't like to do. I'll be recommending places to get work done as cheaply as $5. With $50 or $100 you can put together a very nice book and get started selling – while you may not have $100 to spare, I'll bet you know someone who can loan it to you. Or you can find a way to make a little extra money. Or you can cut costs for a month and save it. Although it's not required, having a little bit of budget can save you a lot of time and frustration.

On the other hand, if you're going to be publishing lots of books, or a series, it's best to learn some of the software and process so that you can have more control and do more things yourself.

MY STORY

When I first started publishing over a decade ago my books were homemade and pretty ugly. Although I was thrilled and proud of them, poor reviews and slow sales caused me to reevaluate. For later books I increased my budget to get everything professionally done. Even though they did very well in their particular niche (I got some reviews from famous people, featured in mainstream magazines and sold international rights), the readership numbers were low and the books were never meant to be bestsellers. I finally realized the books I was writing had a limited market.

So I put writing on hold for a while. I finished my MA and started my PhD in English Literature, supporting myself with an online editing service I founded. Later that transitioned into book cover design, and I now offer a wide range of author services. Through my work with indie authors, I've learned a lot about book design, book marketing and promotion, and publishing in general. But I knew to really build up my credibility and have people take my advice seriously, I needed to focus on writing my own books and hitting the big sales numbers that all authors covet. I'm going to do that by putting out ten books in 2014, including short how-to guides like this one, trade fiction and non-fiction, and some more specialty books on creativity, philosophy, literature and other topics that interest me.

At the same time I'm growing my platform with my blog and by putting out a lot of practical tools and information to help authors publish. I'm not in the big leagues yet, but I do make my living online and an increasingly large chunk of my income comes from book sales. My wife and I enjoy travelling and are semi-migratory; roaming the world in search of beautiful places and interesting experiences. Now that I'm dedicated to producing my own content, I plan to hit a million downloads in the next few years (or at the very least, publish over 1 million words – I'm at about 350,000 right now). Stay tuned if you want to learn how it all unfolds.

In 2013 I put out a short guide to my thoughts on book marketing called Book Marketing is Dead – since a lot of my clients and readers were asking me how to promote their books. Reviews have been favorable except on two issues.

Some people thought the services I suggested were too expensive (even though they were pretty cheap compared to everything else out there). Other people thought my tone was too negative. In that book I stressed that only good books that had been turned into professional projects had a chance at success. I warned that most indie-published book covers were ugly, and most homemade author websites would scare readers away. I emphasized these things because they will make the biggest impact on sales, and your book won't be successful if nobody buys it.

On the other hand, spending a lot of money on your book – especially your first book – is not really a good idea. In the entrepreneurial world we have terms like "minimal viable product" or "validation of ideas." It's smart, and ultimately much less frustrating, to test out whether a product has a market before you invest a lot of money in it.

The same is true of books (although it's a little more complex). Basically, you want to spend as little as possible publishing your book the first time around, and put it out into the world, so that you can see if anybody actually pays money for it – and whether it gets good reviews. Once you've sold some copies to strangers and they've really liked it, you'll know your book has potential, and you can spend a little more if you want.

But there's another reason not to spend much on your self-published book. A lot of authors who have some budget choose the middle ground: they don't want to do everything themselves so they sign up with a small press or self-publishing service. These services charge a few thousand dollars but help put together the formatting and book cover design, as well as organizing all the files and getting them in the right places. While this may be easier, and it may seem like a step up from doing everything yourself, it rarely is. That's because small presses or author publishing services usually don't have a design team with the talent to make your book as amazing as it should be, and they often farm out the work to cheaper providers. About half of my clients sign up with services like these to make their lives easier, but they hire me to do the cover design anyway because they didn't like the provided cover, and then they complain that the formatting isn't very good either.

At this point I'd usually offer to help out with the formatting, taking over the project and spending a lot of my own time; volunteer activities like this made me so busy I had to shut down my site for four months just to catch up with all the work. (Since then I've hired a full-time formatter to help out so I can focus on cover design).

The fact that authors have limited options for producing a high quality book, and that even paying a lot of money won't guarantee that the cover design and formatting is professionally done, led me to develop some tools and resources to make it easier for authors to design their own books without making the mistakes that will kill sales. I strongly believe that, if you do things yourself, you can save money and produce a better quality product that will sell more books.

Finally, the strategy that seems to have the best chance for success right now is to publish a bunch of shorter stories rather than big long novels. So you need a way to publish lots of content, quickly, without spending time and money. This book should help make that process easier.

PART ONE

Write

Writing a book is a

HORRIBLE, EXHAUSTING STRUGGLE

LIKE A LONG BOUT WITH SOME PAINFUL ILLNESS

ONE WOULD NEVER UNDERTAKE SUCH A THING

if one were not driven on by some demon

WHOM ONE CAN NEITHER RESIST NOR UNDERSTAND

GEORGE ORWELL

WRITE

> "When I write, I feel like an armless,
> legless man with a crayon in his mouth."
> —Kurt Vonnegut

Writing a book is not supposed to be easy. The good news is, it gets easier. The trick is to push through with the first one, then start the next. There are tons of resources available to authors wanting to write a book, but in my experience it always comes back to the actual process of getting the words done on paper, then revising and editing and organizing, that authors get stuck on.

You need to actually put your butt in the chair for 100+ hours and write paragraphs until the whole damn thing is finished. The first draft may be exciting and fun – until you figure out that the writing isn't so great, and the book needs a lot of fixing and tweaking. This discovery can be quite a blow. Learn to expect it: the first draft is not going to be stellar. But you still need to get it down, so that you have some material to work with.

"You have made some notes, read some writing books, and done some research. Mostly what you've done is talk about writing a book. An idea for a book is not a book; it is a waste of time. There is no singular thing that makes someone a writer, but there is one thing that makes someone a joke—talking about writing a book without doing any work." —Pat Walsh,

78 Reasons Why Your Book May Never Be Published

So before we talk about formatting, publishing and promoting, let's focus on the core.

WHAT SHOULD I WRITE ABOUT?

I'm going to tell you something that you're not going to like: not all books will be successful. Even a well-written book will only be as successful as the number of people interested in reading it. If you follow my blog you know I don't believe in the "follow your passion" or "do what makes you happy" philosophy. I don't believe you were put on this earth to write the one PERFECT book. In fact, I think that's a terrifying belief, and most likely the root of your inability to get it done. You're probably a smart and capable person and there's no end to the kinds of books you could write. But there is a huge difference in what kinds of books are likely to be successful.

Recently I was chatting with a friend of mine who plans to write a fantasy trilogy after he finishes his PhD. He's been thinking about it for decades. It's his one true passion. The trouble with writing is, the more you care about the book, the harder writing it will be. You'll obsess and get frustrated and not be satisfied. You'll revise and rewrite and add and remove. You may spend years on it. It's much easier to learn to write well if you begin by cutting your teeth on side projects that you don't care as much about. That way you can make it a game and not take it so seriously. You can have more fun. Perhaps every author needs to give birth to his own true love before they are ready to move on to other projects; but something successful authors learn in retrospect is to consider what kind of books are actually selling.

If you like writing, and you want to make a living with it, deciding what kind of books to write will boost your chances of success by an amazing degree. How many copies a month would you like to sell? 100? 1,000? (In other words, if you're profiting $1 per sale, would you rather make $100 or $1000 extra dollars a month?) That's not an insignificant difference. If you write 10 books, the choice becomes: would you rather make $10,000 a month or $100,000 a month?

You can choose what kind of book to write, and some genres have 10X as many active readers. So it makes sense to try and write a book in a popular genre, rather than writing the book that you really want to write.

"Writing is like sex. First you do it for love, then you do it for your friends, and then you do it for money." —Virginia Woolf

"Isn't that selling out!?" you cry in horror. But the truth is, publishing success is a numbers game. It's about your own productivity (how many books) versus the available readership (people who like to read those kinds of books).

Books X # Readers = $$$

You want high numbers in both fields.

This will probably rub you the wrong way, so I'll give you some extra reasons to adopt this thinking.

1. Your first book probably won't be very good.
2. The book you care about most is the hardest to write.

I have a novel in me that I care about passionately. It's everything I want to say in this life. I LOVE it, but the available readers are not huge, and even if it's awesome, it probably won't be a huge success. But because I care about it so much, I can't finish it. I've rewritten it several times, redone chapters, made up new characters… it's an evolving, never-ending process. I even pitched it to agents and had some call me back, but then I realized how far it was from finished and backed out. I've learned a lot about writing from that (so-far) failed novel.

The more you care about the result, the less you'll be able to finish it. I'm not suggesting your book idea isn't amazing, simply that you should improve your writing skills first on projects you care less about, that you have less emotional dependency with. Save your Big Idea for after you've developed your writing skills, so that you can do the one that really matters to the best of your ability. Writing is a skill that improves with practice; if you were a carpenter, you'd be proud of your very first table, even though the quality would most likely be poor. It doesn't mean you're a bad carpenter or that it's a bad table. After 100 tables you'll start getting really good at it, and your business will finally take off.

If you've already finished a novel – fine, put it out there and see how it goes. But even if it's wonderful, it's unlikely you'll be very successful with only one book. You may need to write several books before people notice that first book – and then it'll finally catch on. Those rules are true about 90% of the time.

In the history of literature, most great writers wrote books that didn't do so well before writing something with more popular appeal. Stephen King wrote Carrie to get in on a wave of possession-horror books during the "Satanic Panic" of the 1970s. Stephanie Meyer wrote an alien romance before turning to the more popular vampire genre with Twilight. Hugh Howey was working on other projects before putting out the first segment of Wool – connecting with the wildly popular dystopian genre. Suzanne Collins wrote the Underground Chronicles before beginning the Hunger Games. Cormac McCarthy was already famous before beginning The Road to cash in on the post-apocalyptic genre. My point is that, even established authors turn to more popular genres to make a bigger impact and sell more books. Huge global successes are in a very tight group of popular genres. The question shouldn't be "What do you want to write?" but "Would you rather sell 100 copies or 100,000 copies?"

If you are writing in a less popular genre, don't be surprised when you have much lower sales and face more difficulty in connecting with readers and marketing your book. It's not you; it's only that you've written something without considering how many people out there will want to buy it.

> "The big trinity of publishing: mystery, thrillers and romance. If you can combine all three, then it's a winner's trifecta and you'll be rich beyond your dreams." —Dermot Davis,
> Brain: The Man Who Wrote the Book that Changed the World

I spent my 20s writing books I wanted to write and marketing my surrealist oil paintings, but it was always an uphill battle. Then I realized it was ultimately selfish to create whatever I wanted and expect others to buy it. Now I believe in making things of value to other people by doing things I enjoy anyway, like writing.

You can make a lot of money writing. But you have to produce quickly, and you have to publish often, and you can't waste years trying to finish your one perfect book. If it's really important to you, leave it for a few years, write 10 bad books first instead (you'll learn a lot in the process), start earning some passive income, and then return to it when you have the talent and resources available to do it really well.

Personally, I like making money. I find my life is much happier and more enjoyable when I don't have to worry about income all the time. Most authors will never make enough money from their books to quit their jobs; which means they'll never really have the free time to devote themselves to writing. I follow one such author on Facebook, and it's really sad to see how, even though he's built a big platform and had some successful books, he has trouble paying bills and keeping up with his mortgage. Sometimes he sounds a little desperate, asking for donations from his fans to keep his head above the water.

I have another friend who outsources book production to his team in the Philippines. They do the research, write the books, edit them and do the design. He has hundreds of little books on niche topics. They aren't anything amazing, but he makes over $10,000 a month.

If you want to write for the "Art" of it and keep financial concerns completely separate, that's your choice. You may have deep-seated beliefs about creativity that aren't easy to amend. I'm not telling you those beliefs are wrong, just that they're inconvenient if you hope to be successful and sell a lot of books.

Maybe you're retired and live in a big house, and making money doesn't matter to you... but money is just an easy measurement to measure the success of a book. No money means nobody is reading it, nobody is sharing or reviewing it, it's not making an impact. Why spend so much time creating something that doesn't matter to anybody? I'm not saying you should "sell out" – but if you're going to spend the time writing something, consider the target market and design a product that they will buy.

"I have to declare in all candor that no one interested in being published in our time can afford to be so naive as to believe that a book will make it merely because it's good."
—Richard Curtis, Notting Hill

"Publishing is a business and writing is an art. The two have to be crammed together despite the clearly different motivations behind them."
—Michelle M. Pillow, Dragon Lords

THERE'S NO "I" IN AUTHOR

If you're publishing a book, you're already in the entertainment business. You need to write for other people if you are expecting them to like it and pay for it. Chris McCullen, author of A Detailed Guide to Self-Publishing on Amazon, has an article called "There's no "I" in author" where he says,

> "As an author, I write primarily for you, not for myself. There are many forms of writing where I can write primarily for myself. If I wish to write only for myself, I would keep a private journal or diary. If you wish to have others read your writing, then don't write just for yourself. Putting little or no effort into editing and formatting is selfish. Making a concerted effort to improve these benefits your potential audience (some of whom may screen your Look Inside for this). Not bothering to learn the basic rules of writing and punctuation (or finding an editor who does) is selfish. Learning the rules, and then only breaking them when you have good reason for it, is something your audience desires. Writing without first researching the expectations of a genre is selfish. Learning these expectations and understanding the reasons for them helps you write a book that fits an audience."

Unless you're a fan of Ayn Rand (I am, incidentally), most people will shy away from accepting the label of selfishness. And although most of us also refuse to participate in genuine Buddhist/Christian selflessness – absolute charity and good works with no personal possession, authority or gain – we still collectively appreciate the idea of selflessness as a moral height towards which to aspire.

We hold these vague moral contingencies with relative absolutism... until we get into the sphere of creativity. The "Follow Your Passion" ideology demands we ignore others and create only for our true self. It mono-maniacally vetoes any indication of compromise; if you think about the end users, the consumers, the market, the money – you've already sold out and all your work, and your core self as well – is automatically deemed trivial, empty, shallow and worthless.

Here's just one popular quote (out of hundreds) to illustrate what I mean:

Better to write for yourself and have no public,
than to write for the public and have no self.
—Cyril Connolly

Artists and creators love quotes like these. They give you permission to do whatever you want and not give a crap about anyone else. Freeing yourself from inhibition or fears about what other people will think is necessary to get started; but creating things for yourself and hoping they will become successful is like buying a lottery ticket. It might work out, but it probably won't. Why does it have to be so black and white? Why can't I write for myself and the public (I'm a very capable person, after all).

It may seem like I'm preaching, or that this stuff "doesn't matter." But the truth is, the number of readers for the genre you decide to write in will have an enormous impact on your sales, so don't take it lightly.

"It's not actually about writing what you want as an indie. If you want success, you have to focus on your readers, and if you want faster success, you should keep satisfying that core group of readers as that will bring you organic growth through word of mouth."

—Steena Holmes, The Memory Child

LET'S GET STARTED

So let's say you agree with me and you're ready to crank out a quick book that will make some money. A test-run, if you will. How do you know what to write? How do you know what will sell? How do you find the time and motivation to get it done?

What kind of book to write =
Genre + Format + YOU

It's probably easiest to start with a genre you like (but maybe not… if you pick something else that you don't care about much, it may be easier not to take yourself so seriously). Make it fun. Make it a game. Don't worry about making it a good book. Your only goal should be to finish it. Start by doing your research.

"Read, read, read. Read everything - trash, classics, good and bad, and see how they do it. Just like a carpenter who works as an apprentice

and studies the master. Read! You'll absorb it.
Then write. If it's good, you'll find out. If it's
not, throw it out of the window."

—William Faulkner

Read the top 10 bestsellers in your chosen genre. After each one, make a one page plot summary. What happens? Make a brief timeline. When you finish the 10 books, find the elements they have in common. For example nearly all YA (Young Adult) Paranormal Romances go something like this:

1. Hero/Heroine is uncool, unnoticed.
2. Parents died or are missing.
3. Discovers secret powers/ability/unique history.
4. Has a friend of the opposite sex who wants more from them, but they aren't interested "in that way."
5. Has a romantic interest split between two ideal people, both really want him/her – one is "safe" and one "bad."
6. Often a secret war or struggle going on, where they discover they have a unique role to play.
7. They discover something shocking about their parents.
8. The bad guy usually turns out to be the father, mother or uncle.
9. They are scared of their powers and begin to think they might be bad or evil.
10. Build up to the "final battle" or the face-to-face conflict, but the bad guy gets away so the story can continue in the next book.

If you plan to write a paranormal romance, you would start with a list like that. You'd throw in some background of your universe (what kind of powers do they have? What's the history? Where did the conflict start) but then you'd add in your UNIQUE history.

"Write what you know" means taking scenes and experiences and knowledge from your own life and putting them into your book.

Take each of your characters and have a personal acquaintance (someone you like or hate) to model them after. Take each scene and think of a specific place you've been to. If you have an interest in knitting, so does the heroine. If you used to work at a summer camp, take those skills/setting and put them in the book. Put as much of YOU as you can, without making it boring. This will add detail and authenticity – and it will be so much easier to write.

A WORD ON POINT OF VIEW

Another reason I may have been unable to finish that novel of mine is because I kept trying to use 3rd person – "He said…" I thought I needed it to handle the scope of the novel and all the different characters. But it's tough to start writing that way without practice, and my writing showed it. Luckily, most of my favorite best-selling books (especially in the genres I like) write in first person. And first person is easy.

Have you ever kept a journal? I have – I've been doing it for decades. Which means I've gotten really, really comfortable writing in first person. All I need to do is pretend to be the main character and write naturally. So if you're considering the decision on which point of view to take, consider that first person may make it 10X easier for you to write and finish the book. In which case, the question is really "What's better, finishing the book or not finishing?" Though this may not be true for you, I think most people will feel most comfortable with first person, so at least try it out.

This is also true for non-fiction writers. 3rd person is boring. If you want people to enjoy your non-fiction, you need to give it action and a story by telling it in first person. You need to discuss how you discovered the problem, then the solution. You need to organize your material like a story.... "I went to visit this professor... he sat on his polished mahogany desk wearing a red velvet jacket and black frame glasses, eating macaroons." You need to make it vivid in detail, and sneak in all the "information" in between "scenes."

MAPPING IT OUT

Once you've got your notes, map it all out, scene by scene. In the book 2,000 to 10,000, Rachel Aaron's major takeaway tip is that planning your book in detail drastically improves writing speed. Sean Platt recommends "story-beats" – or an outline of all the big events – in Write, Publish, Repeat. Make an outline. Think about how you want each scene and chapter to begin and end. Always note the reason that any character does anything (and don't rely on luck, coincidence or Deus ex Machina.) Plan out your revelations and twists. You may feel this is unnatural for you, but if it increases your writing speed and helps you finish the book in one pass (rather than having to significantly rewrite major changes later) it's well worth it.

If you don't know anything about the "Hero's Journey" or the "Three Acts" you need to do some studying. All good stories have the same elements and are arranged the same way; human beings have been programmed to respond to certain psychological story-telling triggers for thousands of years – don't shrug it off and think "my story is different, I don't need that rigid structure." In

Write Your Novel From the Middle (which you should read so you can discover more about the essential moment in the middle of every story) James Scott Bell says you have to translate your story into a form that readers can relate to, and "That's what structure does. To the extent that you ignore it or mess with it, you risk frustrating – or worse, turning off – readers... Manuscripts that ignore structure are almost always filed under Unsold."

WHERE TO WRITE IT (SOFTWARE AND WEB SOLUTIONS)

I remember coming home to my parents' house one year during college to find that they'd reformatted my hard-drive. They "thought" they'd saved all my data on floppy disks, but alas, no. Gone were the years of journal entries, the short stories and half-finished manuscripts, and what felt like a piece of my soul.

You'd think I would have learned my lesson... I didn't start using a backup service until this year (I'm using BackBlaze); concerned about how devastating lost client files would be for my business. And when my external hard-drive started making a loud ticking noise, I copied everything over to a new one.

Unfortunately, since it seemed to still be working, I kept using it for a few more weeks, haphazardly saving to one hard-drive or the other. I knew it was dumb, but I was too busy to sort it all out.

When it died completely, I was lucky to have the bulk of everything backed up; but during that crucial 2 weeks of overlap, my Backblaze software wasn't running, because it had been set to my previous installation of Windows and I'd re-installed Windows to fix some other problems. I needed to reset Backblaze to set up my current installation, but the instructions were confusing, and I didn't follow through until I'd already lost the drive.

Although I didn't lose anything major (except a few weeks of work I needed to redo) the most painful loss was the novel I'd just starting writing. Losing the first chapter of the first book in what I'd planned to be a very productive 2014 was crippling to my motivation.

Sure I could just rewrite it, and the new version may actually be better than the original, but the frustration of it robbed me of the burning enthusiasm I'd cultivated. The lesson in these events that I mean to strongly impress upon you is that you should be writing online or using something that backups automatically (and infallibly).

Nothing is more important than preserving your writing. There are a lot of methods, but I use Dropbox – something I was already familiar with and had on my computer. I just have a folder in my Dropbox that says "My Writing" where I keep all my books and projects – that folder has a shortcut on my desktop, so I can use it like a normal folder, but the contents are all automatically backed up online.

There are several "write your novel online" sites like Litlift.com, Hiveword.com, or Nownovel.com, and they have promise if you can get used to them. Amazon's StoryBuilder is interesting, and there's also offline software like PlotBuilder, and NewNovelist. Besides backing up files, a major benefit of good writing software is that it helps you structure your story in the right way. Dramatica Pro, for example, based on the firm structure, characterization and plot development of classical literature helps you organize your writing in a specific format. While it taught me a lot about organizing and writing a novel, I still found it too methodological and restricting for actually getting the writing done. I tend to think of writing software as training-wheels; essential for first-time writers who need to learn the skills quickly, but less useful if you've assimilated the lessons. (If you want to bypass the software, you can just read a dozen books about writing from your local library. Still... I'd recommend Dramatica Pro for any hopeful author).

Lots of writers love Scrivener as a writing platform, for a variety of reasons (mostly the session word-count goals and the ability to move sections around).When I started writing this book, I was anti-Scrivener. I preferred MS Word, which was familiar enough not to be distracting. "Writing software can help you organize all your notes and information, but too much planning and plotting (while it's important and will definitely improve the final book) can actually get in the way during the process," I argued.

But this week I started writing a new novel and today I spent a couple of hours getting used to Scrivener. I believe I'm now a new convert. Previously, I'd organize several Word documents with research and notes, and try to keep a "clean" file for the actual writing, but there were lots of duplications and I was always saving "newer" files. There would also be a lot of scrolling up and scrolling down to find the information I wanted.

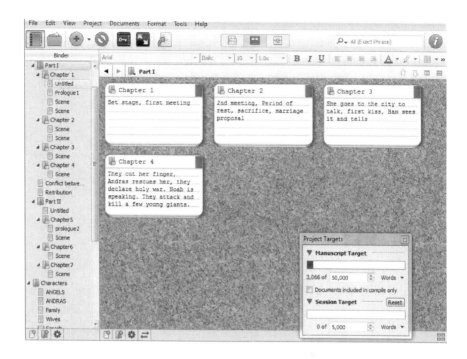

In Scrivener, I can set up all the sections and divide them between chapters and scenes; then I can make quick notecards so I know what needs to happen, and I can add the research down under the Characters, Places or Research tabs.

That helped me map things out much better and solve some major plotting problems before I actually started writing. I like the "Project Target" window that I can reset to hit a target for each writing session. And I like the full screen mode that removes all the menus and darkens the background, so I can just focus on the writing. So, while I've always gotten by without it (and even been resistant to using it), I can understand now why so many writers list Scrivener as their #1 book writing tool.

Whether or not you decide to use Scrivener, you need to be comfortable enough with what happens, who the characters are, how they feel, what the scene looks like to bang out a chapter without stopping to do research or look at your notes. The whole thing should have happened in your head a dozen times; you should be dreaming about it already. So all you need to do is let it out.

If you need to look up something later or forgot a specific detail, just write XXXX and come back to it during the revision process.

Write the book. No fancy stuff. Write it quickly. Every night read what you've written and prepare for the next part. If you get "stuck" it's because there's a problem with your story. But you'll find, once you're writing, that your creative brain continues to play with the story all day long, whether you're taking a walk or doing the dishes. If you have a problem, don't worry about it, just relax and trust that your amazing mind will figure things out.

"Start writing, no matter what. The water does not flow until the faucet is turned on."
—Louis L'Amour

Let yourself explore and go deeper. You should have an idea of where you want to end up, and what basically happens, but often the best parts are character tangents or pieces that came out of nowhere. Get into the flow and let the words appear.

"It was only after two years' work that it occurred to me that I was a writer. I had no particular expectation that the novel would ever be published, because it was sort of a mess. It was only when I found myself writing things I didn't realise I knew that I said, 'I'm a writer now.' The novel had become an incentive to deeper thinking. That's really what writing is—an intense form of thought."

—Don DeLillo

SPEAKING YOUR BOOK

A friend of mine, Sean Fiedel, wrote a book called "How To Write A Book Without Typing It in 6½ Easy Steps." In it he encourages writers to use voice-recognition software to write their first draft quickly. I haven't spent much time experimenting with this but I can see how, especially for non-fiction but potentially for fiction as well, speaking it all out loud could by-pass your inner critic and let you get a rough draft out quickly, which you could then revise and improve.

SET A FIRM DEADLINE OR WORD COUNT

Writing a book could take years, or you could finish it in less than a month. It's important to have clear goals and deadlines. Many successful writers use a mandatory daily word count, and they don't stop, relax or do anything else until they've hit it. Hitting small "success" goals like this can build confidence, increase motivation and get you "on a roll" towards finishing. As a chronic procrastinator (or as I like to call it, someone who does their best work under pressure) I believe in public deadlines. I'll make my cover design and start talking about it, and let people know I'm working on it and when it will be ready. Having people waiting on or expecting the book keeps me on task. I'll also look for a big event to join – a date by which I need to have a physical copy in my hands so I can share it with people.

This year I'm flying back to Portland, Oregon for the summer (from Taiwan) and attending the "World Domination Summit" – a three day business, blogging and lifestyle conference founded by Chris Guillebeau. Since it's a major event, if I want to connect with any bloggers or friends who can review my books, they've really got to be finished. It's already April 17th, 2014… I need to finish this book so I can start working on my next two projects in earnest. That gives me about 5 weeks each for the next two, or at least 10,000 words a week (those books should be considerably longer, but a lot of it is research). It's a little stressful, sure, but the pressure keeps me on task. If I can only finish one of the books before that deadline in July, I have another deadline in October – a big entrepreneurial conference in Bangkok.

DEALING WITH WRITER'S BLOCK

I'll let you in on a little secret: I don't believe in writer's block. I do think it's hard to write something you don't know enough about. And I believe our subconscious minds refuse to let us work on something we know isn't a good idea. So if you're stuck, it might be because you don't know what really happens in the scene or why it happens. Or you're trying to make the characters do something they don't want to do. Or you're trying to write a scene that doesn't make any sense. Or there's a big problem with the beginning of your book and you don't know how to go back and fix it all. That's why you get stuck: you're doing something wrong. Motivation isn't the problem, so stop beating yourself up over "not writing." Telling yourself you MUST write is like driving on a flat tire. Don't do it.

Stop the car, get out, look for the problem, and fix it. Although you don't want to do serious editing or critique at this point, if your book breaks down and you can't go on, it's OK to go back and fix something – even roughly – so that you can continue with the story.

It doesn't matter if, at first, you can't find the solution. Your brain works on whatever challenges you are facing. Give it a task and then move on to something else, and it will solve itself.

The only thing you need to do if you get stuck is find the problem. What is my subconscious trying to tell me? Why do I have these uncomfortable feelings about my work? Rework your plot outline and get feedback from some friends to see if they have questions. Once you identify the problem you need to solve, let it percolate. The answer will come when you least expect it.

> "The best time for planning a book is while you're doing the dishes."
> —Agatha Christie

Most other people at this point would recommend Steven Pressfield's The War of Art or Brené Brown's Daring Greatly: two books that encourage creatives to ignore their inner voices of "Resistance" or "Shame." If self-doubt is your major problem, those books could help. But I don't think it's your problem. In my view, the Follow Your Passion ideology which focuses on creation but refuses to acknowledge the importance of commercial success or viability automatically breeds self-doubt and insecurity. If you create something while refusing to think about who will read it or whether it will be popular, of course you will lack confidence. The only protection you have against fears that it will be a total failure is faith that this is worth your time even if nobody likes it and it isn't a commercial success.

In any other line of work or business, thinking about earning a return on your time and investment is practical. But because of inspirational Follow Your Passion gurus, writers and artists are taught to ignore the practical financials and create from the heart (which more often than not leads to failure, which leads to doubt and insecurity, which leads to bestselling books about how to push through insecurity and produce anyway).

Although I mistrust the philosophical platform behind it, on a practical level I know these ideas have helped a lot of writers to overcome resistance or fear and finish their book. I'm not saying they are flat out wrong: but they only help you finish the work, they don't help you create the kind of work that will be successful. If you happen to make something that will resonate with people, lucky for you. I choose to figure out what will resonate before I start, to save a lot of time. Still, you won't always feel like writing and you will make excuses sometimes. Instead of getting frustrated or disappointed with yourself, externalizing your fear or resistance as an evil force in the universe trying to keep you from producing lets you off the hook, and also neutralizes any rational self-talk. There are no excuses.

Elizabeth Gilbert (author of Eat, Pray, Love) introduces a similar technique in her TED talk, "Your Elusive Creative Genius." In it she recommends going back to the more traditional view of genius as an external muse, and making it responsible for creative production. All you can do is sit down and put in the time and the work. But if you get blocked, look over your shoulder (or wherever you imagine your muse is sitting) and say "I showed up for my part of the job. I'm here, but if you want this thing to be successful, you need to do your job." You should watch the talk, it's here: http://www.ted.com/talks/elizabeth_gilbert_on_genius

> "Do plumbers get plumber's block? What would you think of a plumber who used that as an excuse not to do any work that day? The fact is that writing is hard work, and sometimes you don't want to do it, and you can't think of what to write next, and you're fed up with the whole damn business."
>
> —Philip Pullman, The Golden Compass

But on another level, I don't think seeing artistic production as necessarily a struggle between forces of good and evil is healthy or beneficial. We tend to experience what we expect. Personally, I don't experience resistance, fear or shame when I'm writing a book. Instead of expecting them and fighting against them, why not dissolve them through positive thinking and optimism (not to mention, approaching writing as a business so that you have realistic expectations of success which won't lead to disappointment or frustration.)

If you have confidence issues, I recommend listening to Kelly Howell's The Secret Universal Mind Meditation as you go to bed, and starting your days with this "Successful Author" virtual vision board on YouTube.

IF IT'S NOT FUN, QUIT

Most writers will tell you to write even if you're lazy or tired or discouraged. I disagree: if you don't feel like writing, there's an issue you need to address. Maybe you're doing it for the wrong reasons. Maybe you're not really excited about this project. Writing your book should be the most fun thing you can do. It should be more interesting than watching TV. Another great tip from author Rachel Aaron is, "If I had scenes that were so boring I didn't want to write them, there was no way anyone would want to read them. This my novel, after all. If I didn't love it, no one would"(2,000 to 10,000).

So if you feel you have to be motivated to finish a scene that's just "filler" to get to the fun scenes… rewrite. Focus on THIS scene – how can you make it awesome, surprising and funny? Every scene needs to do something, either reveal new information or push the scene forward. Every scene needs to show the characters do something they might actually, naturally do as a response to something that happened earlier. If it's no fun to write, it's no fun to read. Which means, luckily, you can just write the fun stuff all the time, and probably have a pretty successful book.

The same holds true for non-fiction. I love research and the challenge of putting it altogether into a narrative or argument. But I have to care about what I'm saying, I have to believe the information is going to matter to people. I can't get lazy or just do it for money or not care about the quality. I don't write books flippantly. I write them if I believe I know something that might be valuable to other people.

That said, once you've finished the first rough draft, things may get harder. Some authors like C.J. Lyons find the first draft easy, but the revision difficult. Others, like Hugh Howey and

Joanna Penn, find the first draft hard, and are more comfortable revising and editing. It's safe to say that there will be some parts of the writing/revising process that are extremely difficult for you, and you're going to need to do them anyway. Even if you're pretty motivated and productive, every writer has trouble making their books as good as they want it to be.

While the first draft can be thrilling, once you get some constructive criticism and feedback, you may see your book in a new and negative light. It's OK to care enough about the quality of your work to be unsatisfied, but don't let it turn into overwhelming frustration. For me the best way to get through this phase is keeping in mind the "Equal-Odds Rule," summarized by Sebastian Marshall in IKIGAI this way:

- If you want to make excellent stuff, you need to make a lot of stuff.
- If you make a lot of stuff, you'll make a lot of crap.
- If you want to make excellent stuff, you need to make a lot of crap.
- And that's OK, because you are judged by your best work.

You need to write a lot of crap to get something good. So if the voice in your head is getting you down and telling you your book sucks, look up and say "Yeah I know – so what? I've still got to finish it. This is just one of the 9 crappy books I need to write before I have that one bestseller." Then keep writing. This isn't an excuse to write crap, and you should try to make it as good as you can, but not every book can be your best work ever. Do the best you can and let it go.

"I wrote a book. It sucked. I wrote nine more books. They sucked, too. Meanwhile, I read every single thing I could find on publishing and writing, went to conferences, joined professional organizations, hooked up with fellow writers in critique groups, and didn't give up. Then I wrote one more book." —Beth Revis, Across the Universe

"I often think publishing a book is like doing a poo. Once it's ready for the world, you have to relinquish that control and let nature take its course. A few will be impressed by your creation, others will be disgusted. Plus, no one will enjoy your success and achievement in producing it as much as you did." —H.O. Charles, City of Blaze

Another tip I learned from Sebastian Marshall is to put yourself in a group of the most successful writers of all time and consider them your competition. They are just people, not geniuses, and they faced the exact same problems you are having. The only difference is that you are starting out on your journey and need to catch up to them.

"A professional writer is an amateur who didn't quit." —Richard Bach

"The hard part about writing a novel is finishing it." —Ernest Hemingway

It's your job to finish the work, not judge the work. Do the best you can, and if it's bad, just assume you are purging all the bad writing out of your system, and that it's a necessary step to improving your writing that you are required to go through before you begin your real books.

This passage from modernist poet Rainer Maria Rilke highlights similar issues; producing great art may require pain and discomfort. Let it happen, and don't fret about it. Recognize it as a sign that you're on the right path.

"Why do you want to shut out of your life any uneasiness, any misery, any depression, since after all you don't know what work these conditions are doing inside you? Why do you want to persecute yourself with the question of where all this is coming from and where it is going? Since you know, after all, that you are in the midst of transitions and you wished for nothing so much as to change. If there is anything unhealthy in your reactions, just bear in mind that sickness is the means by which an organism frees itself from what is alien; so one must simply help it to be sick, to have its whole sickness and to break out with it, since that is the way it gets better." —Rainer Maria Rilke, Letters to a Young Poet

"The thing that is really hard, and really amazing, is giving up on being perfect and beginning the work of becoming yourself."
—Anna Quindlen

DEVELOP A HABIT

Conventional wisdom says you need to do something for 21 days in a row to build a new habit, so expect the first month of writing to be REALLY HARD and possibly to get almost nothing done. That's OK. The first month isn't really about writing great content. The first month is about building the writing habit – make that your main goal (so, you should leave an extra month schedule in your publishing plan for you to "waste" this way). Get up. Make your coffee. Disconnect the internet. Stare at the screen for an hour. Write what you can. No breaks, no excuses. When you're done, you can cross it off your list for the day.

Use a smartphone Goal Achieving app like "Don't Break the Chain" or "Streaks" – the small action of checking off your daily goal can be a big motivator, there's a list of them here: http://appadvice.com/appguides/show/habit-building-apps

"Don't bend; don't water it down; don't try to make it logical; don't edit your own soul according to the fashion. Rather, follow your most intense obsessions mercilessly."
—Franz Kafka

"The second thing you have to do to be a writer is to keep on writing. Don't listen to people who tell you that very few people get published and you won't be one of them. Don't listen to your friend who says you are better that Tolkien and don't have to try any more. Keep writing, keep faith in the idea that you have unique stories to tell, and tell them.

I meet far too many people who are going to be writers 'someday.' When they are out of high school, when they've finished college, after the wedding, when the kids are older, after I retire . . . That is such a trap. You will never have any more free time than you do right now. So, whether you are 12 or 70, you should sit down today and start being a writer if that is what you want to do. You might have to write on a notebook while your kids are playing on the swings or write in your car on your coffee break. That's okay. I think we've all 'been there, done that.' It all starts with the writing. " —Fantasy writer Robin Hobb

"Anybody can write a book. But writing it well and making it sell — that's the hard part."
—Jay Taylor, The Rise Of Majick

MOTIVATIONAL POSTERS

The walls of my office are literally covered with motivational quotes and posters. I know how important they are, so I've made a whole bunch of them and put high-res versions on my website that you can download and print, including some of the quotes I used in this book. http://www.creativindie.com/motivational-quotes-for-artists-and-authors/

EDIT

"There Are Two Typos Of People In This World:
Those Who Can Edit And Those Who Can't."
—Jarod Kintz

"The first draft of anything is shit."
—Ernest Hemingway

"Substitute 'damn' every time you're inclined
to write 'very;' your editor will delete it and the
writing will be just as it should be."
—Mark Twain

This is a surprise section, but I can't in good conscious skip from writing to formatting. When you finish your first rough draft, you will feel on top of the world. You'll dream of riches and TV interviews and huge payments from Amazon. But you aren't done! You've just got a bare bones story – it's probably about mediocre.

It could do OK if you throw it out there, but it will do much better if you get it professionally edited.

A great editor will flag plot lines that don't make sense, characters acting without motivation, repetitive words or poor word choices, boring sentences, and even whole chapters to cut. They'll get rid of the fluff and garbage and hone the story, to make it fluid and powerful. Then you'll have to rewrite some, repeat the process, and when the story is finally good enough, you can give it to a proofreader to check for typos and spelling errors.

The problem with all that of course, is that editing is boring, pedantic and time-consuming, and the brilliant editors who do the best work charge a lot of money. If this is your first (or second or third) book, unless you have a lot of cash lying around, I wouldn't invest several thousand dollars in editing until you see whether people like the story (the story matters more than the writing; even if an editor makes all the writing powerful and beautiful, it doesn't matter if the story is poor). It's a Catch-22. You may never be successful without a professional editor to improve your writing; but even a perfect, polished manuscript may not sell.

So although it's critically important, I'm not going to recommend you pay for editing (especially since this is a book about publishing on the cheap). Instead, I'll help you self-edit as much as possible with some tips and resources.

The first step is to put the book away for several weeks/ months and do something else. I strongly recommend going to the library and reading everything you can about writing fiction. There are stacks of great books. Learn your craft. Come back to your book with a better understanding of powerful writing.

I worked as a book editor throughout graduate school, during which time I edited over 100 books. Since moving into book design, I grew my editing company and I now manage a team of professional editors. Although I read less indie fiction or "first-draft" books these days, when I do they usually suffer from common rookie writing mistakes. Luckily some of these things are easily fixable.

1. BUILD SYMPATHY FIRST, SHOW YOUR GOOD/BAD CHARACTERS (CONFLICT)

Your book needs conflict, and your main character has to be sympathetic from the beginning. We need to root for, pity and bond with the main character, and hate and loathe the opposition. There must be a villain, or a source of conflict, or a foil—somebody who for some reason makes the protagonist feel bad.

The protagonist should doubt him/herself, so that through the story they can gain self-confidence and existential security.

This needs to be done quickly. No matter how cool the action scenes are, if we don't know who to root for, if we don't feel an emotional connection to the outcome, we just don't care. Before I know which characters are good or evil, when they're all strangers to me, I wouldn't care if any of them got hit by a bus. Which means I'm not invested in your story. Before you blow crap up and have shoot outs, readers need to know, love and care about your protagonist.

2. START WITH THE ACTION

"In many cases when a reader puts a story aside because it 'got boring,' the boredom arose because

> the writer grew enchanted with his powers of description and lost sight of his priority, which is to keep the ball rolling."
>
> —Stephen King, On Writing: A Memoir of the Craft

Almost all scenes/chapters need to start in the middle of the action. Cut out all the lead up stuff. Cut out the explanation, back story, exposition and description of the scene. Start in the middle of a tense dialogue. Start with an attention hooking line. Start with a close-up: zoom in on drops of blood, sweat and tears. Hook attention first – then back up, fill in the details, slow down and set up the next major conflict (then cut the scene and start over with the next one).

At least… that's all true if you're trying to write a bestselling thriller-esque type book. Other books may move slowly and are more exposition, and focus more on scene and emotion. Still, the days of "Call me Ishmael" have given way to "About three things I was absolutely positive: First, Edward was a vampire. Second, there was a part of him–and I didn't know how dominant that part might be–that thirsted for my blood. And third, I was unconditionally and irrevocably in love with him."

Start by grabbing interest and defining the central conflicts; you can fill in the blanks once you have their attention.

3. EMOTIONALLY BELIEVABLE CHARACTERS

Normal people laugh when they're happy. They might be short-tempered and snarky when they are angry. But they rarely "sob hysterically", "shriek uncontrollably", or "shake visibly." People don't let their emotions run wild – especially around a whole group of other people. And they don't flip flop between happy and deathly depressed at every unexpected catastrophe. People usually don't react at all when bad things happen; they are in shock. They hold it in, do what needs done, and only let it sink in when they have time to process their grief. So check how often your main character (or any characters) cry, sob, scream, shriek, etc. You might allow them one emotional display per book (although I wouldn't allow them any). Cut all that crap out, replace it with subtle melancholy, emptiness, inability to experience joy.

4. IT'S/ITS...THERE/THEIR/THEY'RE

It's the easy stuff we tend to miss. Even if we can spell big words correctly backwards, you're going to mess these up a lot: use the search/find feature to search for these one by one and check them all. If you notice something else simple you screwed up, search for it – you probably did it more than once (in one of my books, I used "thrown" for "throne" several times, and readers couldn't stop criticizing me for it). Also, we tend to have 'bad batches' – so if you find any errors, super-edit that section, because there are likely to be more errors nearby.

5. ADVERBS: -LY

"The road to hell is paved with adverbs."

—Stephen King, On Writing: A Memoir of the Craft

Adverbs are bad. They are lazy writing. Any time you express what someone did and how they did it by adding an -ly (said excitedly, left resolvedly, prayed devoutly...) you're missing the chance to use stronger writing and picking something easy instead. A lot of these phrases will be meaningless (like "laughed happily"). Or they will be confusing. So use your search/find button for "ly" and track them all down. Does it need to be there? Is there another way you can show how they did something without using an adverb?

"Said excitedly" = "said, a grin spreading at the corners of his mouth and his body quivering with expectation."

"Left resolvedly" = "stamped out of the room, slamming the door behind him."

Search them out and try to get rid of them all.

6. EXCLAMATIONS

> "Cut out all these exclamation points. An exclamation point is like laughing at your own joke."
> —F. Scott Fitzgerald

Now use the find/replace feature to search for "!" and "?!". People aren't usually very excited, and we don't shout a lot. That means you really don't need to use exclamation points, like, hardly ever. But a lot of indie authors have a bunch of characters saying things like "How dare you!!!" or "Are you crazy?!?!"

Lots of punctuation is no substitute for good writing. Not only is it unnecessary, it's often used to mask over very bad dialogue – so searching for your "!" can indicate poor dialogue that you need to strengthen.

MORE ON DIALOGUE: read it out loud to yourself. Then get two friends to read the script out loud to you so you can hear it. Can they do it naturally, effortlessly, or does it seem fake, false, and forced?

7. ONE SPACE AFTER A PERIOD

I know it's a raging controversy, but I don't care. Use find and replace, hit the space bar twice in the first field, and once in the second field, to replace all your double spaces to single spaces. You don't need any double spaces, anywhere. (Unless you are submitting a manuscript to a publisher/agent, and they specifically request double spacing because it gives them more space for notes – but if you're self-publishing, you don't need them).

When I'm formatting a book, I need to do this step first.

8. NO FANCY WORDS

"Any word you have to hunt for in a thesaurus is the wrong word. There are no exceptions to this rule." —Stephen King

"The most valuable of all talents is that of never using two words when one will do."
—Thomas Jefferson

Unless you're writing a first-person narrative, the narrator should be invisible. So when you use big, strange, fancy, unusual words, it interrupts the action and draws attention to the narrator.

This especially happens with repetition – a novel I read recently used "purchase" in the sense of "to gain traction." The first time I thought it was a bit odd. The second and third time I thought it sounded stupid. You are likely to have favorite words that you like to use, but when you pick a fancy word instead of a common word, it will stand out. Characters themselves can use them in dialogue, but you shouldn't use them in the background (it's like putting a sticker in the book saying "the author of this book is really smart.")

Here's a cool online tool you can use to check the frequency of all the words you used in your book: http://textalyser.net

Just paste all your text there and look at the most common words, to see if you have any bad habits you should break.

If you follow those steps only, your writing will be much better; but keep in mind, editing can't fix a bad story. And a great story will be successful even if the writing is bad!

So make sure the plot goes somewhere, the twists are huge, the dangers and struggles powerful and difficult. Make lots of terrible things happen to the main characters. Don't make things easy for them. Make it a story worth reading. (For non-fiction, make sure it gives a lot of details, it solves a major problem or is full of interesting research).

EDITING NON-FICTION

A lot of these rules hold for non-fiction as well, but I notice different things when I'm editing non-fiction. Non-fiction these days is often a collection of blog articles or separate sections all mixed together with an introduction tagged on.

If this is the case, then your introductions for each chapter will seem incongruous, and your conclusion will be lackluster. When writing non-fiction, the introduction is by far the most important piece. It should lay out your personal motivations for writing the book (your backstory); why this book matters and who it's for; what you aim to prove or demonstrate; and the process you're going to use to get there (chapter summary/outline). If you write the introduction very well, fitting the rest of the pieces together will be much easier.

People love stories, so try to fit in as much personal anecdotes as you can (as long as they are at least mildly interesting, such as meetings with famous people or visits to historical sites). Include stories of other people as well; historical legends, etc. If your non-fiction book is mostly a long rant about your personal opinions, revise heavily.

For more tips on self-editing, check out Polish Your Fiction: A Quick & Effective Self-Editing Guide by Jessica Bell.

GET FREE HELP

If you're in a writer group you may be able to trade editing with other authors. If you have a platform already, some people may be willing to edit your book for free in exchange for you recommending them to other authors (or, just to help out). For my books, I just get it as clean as I can and publish – my friends and fans will probably find all the typos quickly. I go through my books revising, rewriting and editing about a dozen times, so there shouldn't be many; but our brains play tricks on us when we edit our own writing. We know what's supposed to be there, so we often miss what's really there.

PAID SERVICES

If you have the budget for professional editing, check out www. paper-perfect-editing.com – you can submit your manuscript and get a free sample from several different editors and pick the one you like best.

You can also try Fiverr.com, there are a few providers who will edit 1000 words for $5. That's only $500 for 100,000 words (a really good deal). You may get lucky and find somebody amazing, but often low cost providers are just starting out and don't have much experience editing.

If you're not sure if you need an editor (or how 'deep' of an edit you need) email me a chapter and I'll take a quick look. If I can find five typos in five minutes, you're going to want to get it edited.

If it's pretty clean and I can't find any problems, you may be good to go.

UPDATE: Recently I set up a robust editing service for authors who want the best editing money can buy. To promote it, we'll be giving away a free book edit every six months for the next 2 years. To win you just need to write a short article. Give it a shot, you might save a few thousand dollars. www.bookbutchers.com/contest

COVER

"You can't judge a book by its cover but you can sure sell a bunch of books if you have a good one." —Jayce O'Neal

"Thinking about design is hard, but not thinking about it can be disastrous."

—Ralph Caplan

Your book needs a cover, and it's got to be pretty awesome. The cover is your packaging. It's got to attract attention, create a need and make the sale. A good cover will easily double or triple book sales over a mediocre or ugly cover. BUT – you want to publish this book without spending any money.

Before we tackle formatting (where I'm going to recommend you match fonts with the book cover) we've got to figure out how to get you a great looking, but cheap cover.

You can start by reading these two articles I wrote in 2013 that have gotten a lot of traffic:

8 cover design secrets to manipulate readers into buying books

<u>5 common book cover design myths most indie authors believe</u>

To summarize them: use great pictures, use a lot of color and contrast, don't ruin the image with poor text, don't use bevel or drop shadow haphazardly, don't cram too much stuff in, and make them feel epic with really spaced out lettering.

Fiction covers are about the heart. You want an immediate emotional reaction to your cover. This can be done most easily with a beautiful landscape, or with contrasting or rich colors, or by suggesting exciting action. It's also very easy to do with faces and people (especially a person with an emotional look).

Although I don't always love people on covers, and although if you choose a model from a stock photography site there will surely be other book covers using the same model, a cover with a person on it will almost always outsell one without.

A non-fiction book is about the head. You want to capture cognitive attention – usually by blending a couple incongruous things together; a graphic juxtaposition which symbolizes your main idea. It should shock and confuse the brain (trip it up for a moment at least). Once you have their attention, the keyword rich, benefit-driven subtitle is the most important thing on the cover.

The essential thing to remember about a book cover is that its only job is to sell the book. Don't let yourself get distracted or bogged in the creative process of book cover design. The more details you try to micromanage, the worse it will look. Don't choose the cover that you "like" or "feel" is the best one – choose the cover that sells the most copies of your book. If you aren't sure, either test or get feedback. (Not all feedback is the same. Advice from your neighbors, friends and family won't cut it). Keep in mind your end goal: why are you publishing? I hope it's to let a lot of people read and hopefully like your writing, right?

Don't re-invent the wheel. Find a strong cover you like from a best-selling book in the right genre. Don't find 20 that are all totally different. Don't mix and match from 10 (OK you can, but be careful it doesn't look like design porridge). Searching the internet for "best book cover designs" won't work, because those samples are almost always the ones that designers like, not regular readers. They may be cool but are almost always for literary fiction or specialized books, or reprints of classics. You won't find many space westerns or paranormal romance or general spirituality/ inspiration books.

I keep a gallery of covers I see that I like, they may help inspire you. http://bookcovers.creativindie.com/beautiful-book-cover-design-for-inspiration/. You can also view my cover designs on my main site, www.creativindiecovers.com

Find the pictures you want to use. You can browse stock photography sites like 123rf.com, bigstockphoto or depositphotos. You can search DeviantArt for scrap photos that you can use with attribution; same goes for Flickr Creative Commons. If you need to blend a couple together or make them "pop" hire someone on Fiverr.com.

Many authors screw up their covers by thinking of something really complicated, symbolic or conceptual. Stick with people and scenes. Don't focus on a still life or an object (unless there's some action in there somehow). You don't want people to have to think or figure out what the cover means – you've got less than a second to capture their attention.

Pick out the fonts you want to use. In general stick with one fancy font and keep the rest very simple. Don't get crazy. Good clean strong fonts work best. Don't use something fancy for your author name or the subtitle. Put a lot of spacing between the text and between the letters. Don't cover up your beautiful picture.

I put up a post of <u>the 300 best fonts to use for your cover design</u> – that resource may help get you started. You should also download the free package on <u>DIYbookcovers.com</u>; even if you don't end up making your own cover in MS Word (which is very possible, and I'll keep adding resources to make it easier) the guide and instructions will keep you on the right track.

Personally, I'd find a sample cover that was close to what I wanted, pick out the exact fonts I wanted to use, find the most brilliantly amazing picture (the kind that makes your heart skip a beat) and hire someone on Fiverr.com for around $15 to put it all together.

I'm going to put out another guide soon that's more specifically focused on book cover design, in case you're really interested in becoming a book designer, called "Cover Design Secrets to Sell More Books."

Incidentally, this book used to have a different cover. It was clean and professional, "good enough" maybe, but not super. I made a new version, and asked my followers what they thought about it. They overwhelmingly chose the one on the right (which I'm using now). Test covers out and get real feedback. A slightly better cover can make a big difference in sales.

PART TWO

Format

In a badly designed book

THE LETTERS MILL AND STAND LIKE STARVING HORSES IN A FIELD.
IN A BOOK DESIGNED BY ROTE, THEY SIT LIKE

STALE BREAD AND MUTTON ON THE PAGE

In a well-made book

WHERE DESIGNER, COMPOSITOR AND PRINTER

HAVE ALL DONE THEIR JOBS

NO MATTER HOW MANY THOUSANDS OF LINES AND PAGES, *THE LETTERS ARE ALIVE.*
THEY DANCE IN THEIR SEATS. SOMETIMES THEY
rise and dance **IN THE MARGINS AND AISLES**

ROBERT BRINGHURST

THE ELEMENTS OF TYPOGRAPHIC STYLE

FORMAT

"Designers provide ways into—and out of—the flood of words by breaking up text into pieces and offering shortcuts and alternate routes through masses of information. (...) Although many books define the purpose of typography as enhancing the readability of the written word, one of design's most humane functions is, in actuality, to help readers avoid reading." —Ellen Lupton, Thinking with Type: A Primer for Designers: A Critical Guide

"Good design is obvious. Great design is transparent." —Joe Sparano

The dumbest mistake is viewing design as something you do at the end of the process to 'tidy up' the mess, as opposed to understanding it's a 'day one' issue and part of everything."

—Tom Peterson

The following sections on book formatting are a bit technical, so I've made the decision to use screenshots and images, even though these will probably be too small to see clearly in this book. To remedy this, I've put a copy of the text and images online where you can see it better, along with some video-guides and a package of free formatting templates to make things easier. You can find all that at http://www.diybookformats.com

If you don't want to spend any money publishing your book, formatting may seem like any easy thing you can do yourself. It isn't:

1. Formatting is a huge pain in the ass
2. Even after you figure it all out, it won't look professional

Book formatting is actually pretty easy if you know what you're doing – but if this is your first try, you won't do it justice. Designers earn a lot of money, because they know what "looks good" and doesn't look crappy. It's a gift. It's a skill. It's very valuable. They have all the right software and programs, and the expensive computer. It's taken them years of full-time design work to develop their highly trained eyes and style.

But on the other hand, book formatting doesn't require a lot of variation. The majority of books are laid out in a handful of ways, with only a handful of fonts. If you know the right options to choose from, you can't make any big mistakes. Which means it doesn't have to cost a lot of money, because if you know exactly what you want, you can pay a professional for their time – usually a couple of hours – to format your book according to the specs you require.

> "A first-rate story is easily killed by second-rate design." —Mokokoma Mokhonoana, The Confessions of a Misfit

GO GET THE TEMPLATES I MADE FOR YOU

The thing you don't want to do is start from scratch and guess, or do whatever you think looks good. A blank canvas is a writer's worst enemy. Get you started quickly with the free templates I made for you. I've made a version in MS Word and Adobe InDesign. Be careful not to just look at the fonts – one may use a bold Sci-Fi font, so you think "That's it! I want that one!" – but the fonts are easy to change and should match your book cover. You can mix and match different elements, choose what you like, then change the fonts to match your cover. Both the Word and InDesign formats use "Styles" so instead of manually changing fonts on every element, you can change one and update the style, so it will affect all the other instances of the same element.

BUT REALLY, YOU DON'T WANT TO DO IT

Although I want to give you the power to publish as cheaply as possible, I strongly recommend not formatting your own book. Unless you have lots of books to publish (but even then!) formatting is a waste of time, and getting used it, and getting everything right, can easily take up a week of your life. Is it an awesome skill to have? Sure. But somebody else can do it faster and better.

Fiverr.com is my go-to choice for finding formatters. There are many providers who will format your book for Createspace, or for Smashwords, or do InDesign work. $5 is the lowest price, but in my experience an average book will be about $25. Just have the template you want to use ready,and send instructions with what elements and fonts you want to use, and your manuscript. It should take them a couple hours to add the text and style appropriately. If you need to change the book size (my templates are 6"x9") they can do that too.

INDESIGN OR MSWORD?

Both software will give you a PDF file for POD, and they will look pretty much the same (although I made a matching template for both, they aren't exactly the same.) But InDesign will look a little better and cleaner.

CHAPTER ONE

CHAPTER ONE

***

***

LOREM IPSUM DOLOR SIT AMET, consectetur adipiscing elit. Nullam gravida adipiscing velit nec congue. Vestibulum elementum eu dui at fermentum. Nulla dui purus, egestas et eros id, aliquet egestas urna. In ut massa leo. Interdum et malesuada fames ac ante ipsum primis in faucibus. Quisque nisi tortor, consectetur nec nisi sed, pharetra ultricies urna. Nulla sed velit ut justo feugiat semper. Aliquam pharetra fermentum mattis. Curabitur aliquet suscipit ligula, in faucibus ante tincidunt et. Nulla feugiat nulla vel semper dictum. Integer bibendum magna id condimentum porttitor. Mauris dignissim ante at ante congue vehicula.

Cras vel pharetra leo, sed aliquet mauris. Quisque cursus convallis nisl, ac dapibus massa aliquam ac. Donec tempor neque at ante dapibus tristique. Aenean eget mi massa. Ut velit neque, auctor ac sapien sodales, tristique porttitor velit. Mauris vitae lorem eget nibh euismod cursus. Duis pharetra risus ut neque commodo pretium. Praesent suscipit at ligula vitae accumsan. Aenean condimentum aliquam dapibus. Etiam ut justo aliquet, pulvinar tellus sit amet, lacinia arcu. Vestibulum non

Here are a couple examples. MsWord (on the right) can leave big gaps between text, while InDesign does a better job of making the text and spaces even. However, in my experience, the "Final Draft" is never fully clean, and you will always spot a typo or something you want to fix after the book is printed. So if you hire someone to change the InDesign file, you'll need to hire them again to make any fixes.

Whereas, if you hire them to change the Word template file, they'll lay it all out, but you can still make simple changes yourself without having to go back to them all the time. For that reason, I'd probably go with Word, at least the first time around, until you're really sure the manuscript is perfect, and then get someone else to lay it out in InDesign.

If you really want to learn to do it yourself, here's a crash course. If you start from any of the templates, it should save you a lot of time. (As I said earlier, you can absorb this material better on the website I made, so you might want to go bookmark it and then skip over this section.)

www.diybookformats.com

DIY BOOK FORMATTING (WHAT YOU NEED TO KNOW)

If you use the templates I designed, your book will look professional, balanced, aesthetically pleasing and well-spaced. Which means that you'll be getting better formatting at a far lower cost than other alternatives.

But for those of you who want to do more, make more design decisions, possibly even begin offering formatting services, this section will go through some of the basic terms, ideas and options of book formatting.

LET'S START WITH SOME BASIC GROUND RULES

The goal of formatting is to look professional and make the story easy to read. A little bit of style is OK but you don't want to take big risks or do anything strange or distracting. In fact, most of my templates are a bit too flashy (I got bored after the first couple). Using a lot of decorations or fancy fonts is probably a bad idea.

DOING RESEARCH

Go to the library with a ruler. Take pictures of what you like and don't. Browse through my example gallery. Make some decisions. You don't want to play around or hesitate or waste too much time fretting about this stuff. It doesn't matter as much as you think it does, as long as you're copying professionally done books and not making stuff up on the fly.

BOOK SIZE

You'll need to start by choosing a book size. 6"x9" may seem like the obvious choice but for most books I think it's a little big. You don't want a big but very thin book. You want a book that's got some substance and thickness to it. I'd shoot for at least 200 pages, and not more than 350 pages. That's enough to give the book some weight without the printing costs eating into your profits.

If you have a shorter book, say around 50,000 words, this might seem tough to do – but just add in some more spacing (don't make the font sizes bigger). Extra spacing and line height doesn't make a book look cheap, it actually makes it look cleaner and more professional.

You'll need to check your printer / distributor to see what options they offer.

Select One
Industry Standard Trim Sizes
5" x 8"
5.06" x 7.81"
5.25" x 8"
5.5" x 8.5"
6" x 9"
6.14" x 9.21"
6.69" x 9.61"
7" x 10"
7.44" x 9.69"
7.5" x 9.25"
8" x 10"
8.5" x 11"
Custom Trim Sizes
8.25" x 6"
8.25" x 8.25"
8.5" x 8.5"

This is what Createspace offers right now. Of those, I'd start with 5.25 by 8, because the 5×8 cover is too tall and narrow. (A 5 by 8 cover is exactly the "ideal proportions" Kindle wants for cover art – 1.6 – but this is a recommendation all traditional publishers ignore. It may be perfect for an iPhone 5 screen, but on most devices it is ill-fitting.)

The 1.5 ratio of the 6×9 cover is much more "bookish" and ordinary, and leaves more room for cover art. But as I mentioned, 6×9 can feel a bit big and flimsy and I like the smaller, more compact size of the 5.25 by 8.... unless you have a longer book and can pad out a 6×9 to at least a couple hundred pages). Whatever you choose, just set the document size and you're done – it's an easy choice to change later and fix, although you may have to redo some stuff so it's better to decide early.

PAGE MARGINS

The margins are how far the text is away from the edge of the page. You want them to be spacious, but not so much that it seems like you're wasting paper. Half an inch is not quite enough, 1 inch is a little too much.

For the sides, I think between .6" and .8" will do. You can also set the "gutter" – which is the extra space on the edges that are held together in the bending. This brings the text out from the fold a bit. I'm luke-warm on the issue but a .3" gutter will probably do nicely.

neque, auctor ac sapien sodales, tristique porttitor velit. Mauris vitae lorem eget nibh euismod cursus. Duis pharetra risus ut neque commodo pretium. Praesent suscipit at ligula vitae accumsan. Aenean condimentum aliquam dapibus. Etiam ut justo aliquet, pulvinar tellus sit amet, lacinia arcu. Vestibulum non sagittis leo, sed volutpat odio. Cras a dui at quam fringilla consequat. Vestibulum ante ipsum primis in faucibus orci luctus et ultrices posuere cubilia Curae;

Duis at ornare libero. Nunc rutrum volutpat tortor, a faucibus augue congue non. Integer ultricies et magna nec iaculis. Sed tincidunt quis felis vel euismod. Nam pretium elit elementum est ullamcorper dictum. Praesent dapibus dolor ut lorem hendrerit volutpat. Curabitur vulputate placerat turpis at luctus. Suspendisse vel aliquam nulla. Nam tristique sed ipsum eget cursus. Aliquam in adipiscing magna. In quis elit nisi. Donec eu lorem ut nisl adipiscing suscipit eget eu libero.

Maecenas scelerisque felis sed diam pretium, ac adipiscing neque elementum. Quisque mi sapien, tristique et tristique a, euismod vitae lectus. Aenean sed cursus neque. Etiam molestie luctus egestas. Sed molestie iaculis consequat. Quisque euismod erat est, sed vehicula mi convallis viverra. Cum sociis natoque penatibus et magnis dis parturient montes, nascetur ridiculus mus. Cras et odio iaculis, eleifend justo at, pretium elit. Phasellus tincidunt sit amet nibh quis gravida. Quisque auctor aliquet justo et volutpat. Aenean a felis in tortor ultricies feugiat non et eros. Phasellus sapien justo, congue sit amet diam ut, euismod ornare arcu. Proin mollis justo ut nulla lacinia, at pellentesque sem fringilla. Donec vel feugiat odio, vel viverra sapien. Curabitur sed lacus enim.

10

* * *

Cras lectus ante, egestas quis blandit non, mattis quis metus. Vivamus sapien dui, ornare nec massa eget, porttitor gravida tellus. Donec hendrerit posuere placerat. Nulla facilisi. Cras non orci at nisi rutrum sagittis ac congue dolor. Aliquam pellentesque libero sed libero malesuada laoreet. In venenatis dignissim sagittis. Mauris ligula elit, accumsan vel arcu et, dignissim rutrum dolor. Praesent vehicula lacus nunc, sed feugiat ligula semper et. Nunc id massa venenatis magna ornare faucibus quis sit amet arcu. Nam hendrerit mauris vitae urna pharetra lacinia. Aenean blandit nisi quis urna porta, id euismod magna condimentum.

Vivamus non arcu dolor. Integer in pulvinar orci, ac viverra purus. Pellentesque congue eleifend elit, et blandit arcu fringilla sit amet. Nulla blandit neque sed nisi tempus pretium. Aenean lacinia vel mauris sit amet tincidunt. Sed eget quam rhoncus, egestas mi id, facilisis sapien. Donec ut risus pulvinar enim imperdiet suscipit eget vitae lectus.

Vestibulum vehicula tortor ut metus tincidunt, sed feugiat dolor tempus. Class aptent taciti sociosqu ad litora torquent per conubia nostra, per inceptos himenaeos. Aliquam ut erat ipsum. Donec blandit, sem quis adipiscing adipiscing, diam magna laoreet purus, eu gravida dui justo sit amet risus. Nulla varius a libero eget ultricies. Etiam in pharetra augue. Pellentesque dui dui, egestas eu nisi vel, euismod feugiat ante. Sed consequat euismod nisl a sollicitudin. Nunc ac nisl cursus, mollis eros at, imperdiet ipsum. Fusce vehicula neque sit amet tortor

11

Most of my templates are actually set at around .5" ~ .6" margins, and not always with a gutter.

For example, this one (above) has .6" margins on the sides, .55 on the bottom and .65 on the top, with .3 spacing for the header and footer.

Hugh Howey's Dust (set in Adobe Caslon) has about 1" margins and no noticeable gutter. The bottom margin is just under 1", and the headers/page numbers about 3/4th inch from the top margin.

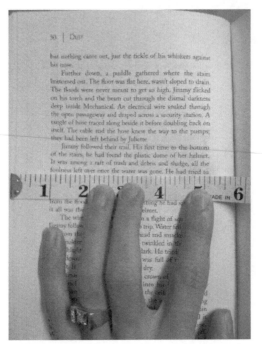

(By the way, I would have gone a font size smaller and added a little more spacing between the lines... Dust is exactly 400 pages, the extra margin spacing and larger size – 6×9 – makes it more hefty and epic, but the font size makes it seem more like a YA book and the line spacing is a little cramped).

Also take into account your headers and footers – they should be roughly evenly spaced between the top or bottom page edges, and the body text. So if your top and bottom margins are .8" (and they should probably be a little bigger than your side margins), then your header or footer would be about .4" in from the edge, with enough spacing between it and the body so it stands out cleanly.

BODY FONTS AND LINE HEIGHT

Unless you're writing a children's book, use a serif font at 11 or 12pt. This is not the place to get creative. You do not need to worry about "sight impaired" people or make your text big and easy to read. The majority of your readers are going to be people who are used to reading regular books.

Use the tried-and-true fonts that are consistently used in print for millions and millions of books. Here's a list of my favorites, in order of preference, and the most common. Some of these have cheaper, common versions – if you can, try to find a "pro" version (if you have to pay for it, it's probably better).

- Adobe Caslon Pro
- Sabon
- Dante
- Minion Pro
- Adobe Garamond Pro
- Goudy Bookletter 1911
- ITC New Baskerville

- Dante
- Minion Pro
- Cardo
- Janson
- Bookman Old style
- Palatino Linotype
- Bembo
- Theano Didot
- Tryst
- Fournier
- Filosophia
- Electra

Check out the computers at your local library or ask your friends to see what fonts they have installed – if they have one you want you can borrow it, or just finish formatting on their computer.

Some fonts look a little smaller than others – Garamond Premiere Pro at 12pt for example looks significantly smaller than some of the other fonts at 12pt. Usually I'd use 11pt or 11.5, but it depends on the size you picked. YA text can be a little bigger (a larger 12) whereas some academic or non-fiction could be a smaller 11.

In general, your line height should be around 1.3.

1 is too tight and 1.5 is often too wide and spread out – although for some genres, especially self-help or spiritual, this extra spacing can really suit the subject matter.

For a 6×9 book, shoot for an average of 350 words per page – for a 5×8, around 300.

But as I mentioned, I firmly believe making the book a little weighty goes a long way in increasing customer satisfaction, so if your print book is under 100 pages for example, I'd increase the line height and margins to push it up closer to 200 pages.

This isn't cheating – people are buying the same book and paying the same money for it. The book will just seem less flimsy or insubstantial.

USING STYLES (IMPORTANT!)

The biggest mistake I see with authors trying to DIY their interior formatting is that they don't use styles.

Both Word and InDesign allow you to set a character or paragraph style – for example, in MS Word, you can click "Header 1" and it will automatically change the font, size, line height, color and spacing.

Formatting.
Let's start with some basic ground rules.

What you don't want to do is decide to change your header font and then go back and have to manually fix every instance. I really hate when an author uses nothing but the default "normal" style – so if I change and update that style it erases everything from all the headers, headings and other elements back to "normal."

SET UP YOUR STYLES FIRST AND REMEMBER TO USE THEM.

Type out a paragraph, set the font, and line height, and remove the indent or set it to "0". Select that paragraph and save it as a style called "Firstparagraph." That's your standard, non-indented first paragraph that's virtually a given in all print books and ebooks (even if you adjust it later, you'll want a first paragraph style that's easy to change).

Copy that paragraph, set the indent to .3" and save it as "normal." That's your regular body paragraph.

MAKE STYLES FOR…
- Chapter-headings
- Subtitle
- Quotes
- Page-numbers
- Title-page
- Copyright-page
- Footers
- Headers

Get those sorted and start using them – that way when the book is all laid out and you decide to change the subtitle font or style, you don't have to go through and fix everything manually, or screw everything up and have to start from scratch.

Instead, you'd just edit one version of the subtitle, highlight it and update the style based on the new settings – and the changes will automatically be made throughout the book (more on the specifics of this later, in the respective software guides).

FRONT MATTER PAGES

You'll want a title page, a copyright page, a TOC (table of contents), preface or introduction, and/or dedication. Both Word and InDesign will let you make an automatic table of contents that you can update without having to do it all manually – those are also important for converting to ebook formats (I'll tell you how to make those later).

CHAPTER PAGES

Chapter pages usually have a little bit of flair and style, depending on the genre, but don't overdo it.

- The body text should start about halfway down the page.
- The top half of the page should be for "Chapter One" or something similar.
- The fonts and style should match your book cover.

You may wish to add a special divider or style but unless you're writing YA romance, conservative is probably best. Simple and stylish.

These are the decisions you have to make:

1. The first paragraph is almost always non-indented; although I've also seen it super-indented.
2. Drop caps on the first paragraph are common, but with or without is fine.
3. All caps for the first few words is common, sometimes in a nice sans-serif for contrast.
4. Chapter pages don't have headers, and rarely page numbers, although a single page number at the bottom (usually centered) is OK – even if the page numbers are usually in the headers on the top of the page.

5. Some books make sure all chapter pages are on the right hand side, leaving a blank page on the left if necessary. But it's not obligatory, and needs more effort.

Word and InDesign are different when it comes to setting up these pages so I'll talk more about that later. For me personally, I just style one chapter page and the first few pages of the book, and then outsource for Fiverr.com for someone to copy my style and finish it up.

YET ANOTHER WORD OF CAUTION…

I didn't want to throw up a bunch of minimalist templates, so I made mine with some kick. But while they may work for YA or Children's books, it's probably best to go even simpler. If you use a fancy Drop cap, don't also use page decorations or a fancy font for the chapter titles. Pair something stylish with something uber-minimalist (a very small, simple serif). Most of my chapter headings are also much too big and bold. Compare my templates with all the ones on the Gallery page of http://www. diybookformats.com to get a sense of what I'm talking about – almost all of them look the same apart for the "decisions" I listed above. Small, simple, stylish, lots of space, fonts that match the cover font – decoration can be fun if used well and sparingly.

SECTION BREAKS

Sometimes a chapter will have different sections, and you want to add a break without using a full on new chapter heading.

You can skip a couple spaces.

You can non-indent the first sentence after the break, or make it bolded or all-caps. A Drop cap is probably over-doing it, but sometimes a slightly larger first letter looks nice.

If you choose a divider, choose carefully.

I've come to realize that I'm not a fan of the very common, three asterisks:

* * *

I think three large periods is more stylish, especially for non-fiction:

• • •

If you're writing romance or fantasy you can use a flourish:

But for most books, I find the little glyphs or symbols more distracting than not. Keep them small and as subtle as possible. Get something custom made that really matches your book.

Or play it safe, and just add a space and a non-indent.

Tip: if you want a really easy way to add something unique, search for symbol fonts, that add symbols or flourishes rather than letters. That way you can just type the symbol, center it and use it just like text. Here's a list of some you can use: Fraktur-Schmuck, Swinging, TheFrench, Tribalism Free, WWDesigns, artistic swash, Calligraphic Frames, ccdiv, ccdiv2, Cornucopia Caligrafica, Destiny's Decorative, Floral Garnish, Floreale Two, NeoclassicFleuronsFree, NatVignetteOne (and Two), Nymphette.

SOMETHING TO WATCH OUT FOR...

Be careful when you center things like chapter headings or break symbols – there's a good chance you're starting from the "normal" style that includes an indent. So you're "centering" it but it's really adding in the .3" indent, which makes the center a little off. If you add section symbols or other centered text, make sure it's set to "0" indent, then center it, then save or update the style.

HEADERS AND FOOTERS

You can also use your headers of footers to cement your book's unique style.

In general, use the book cover fonts (or subtitle/author name fonts if the title font is too messy or unclear). You basically want a simple serif or sans-serif, although italics can look nice too. Page numbers and headings should be a bit smaller, probably 9 or 10pt).

Often left and right pages alternate, so that the text and page numbers are always on the outside edges.

Often one page will have the author name, the other the title.

The text is often in all-caps.

The page number can be up next to the text in the header – if so you can remove some of the footer space or bottom margin.

Or, the page number can be on the bottom.

Having headers and footers centered, rather than at the edges, seems to be pretty common as well – so if figuring out whether you need to align them right or left is getting confusing, there's nothing wrong with centering them all so you don't have to worry one page will be screwed up and ruin the book.

Out of hundreds and hundreds of books I researched, I found a couple with headings on the bottom (which I hate – as I also hate Windows 8 for trying to do the same thing) and one with the headings and numbers on the side margins (interesting, but why try so hard to be different?)

Remember, risks distract from the story and can rarely improve the experience. The story is what matters. The vast majority of books keep it very simple, with the exception of some kids' books and YA fiction.

The job of the formatting is to disappear and use convention to present the story in a format readers recognize and expect, so they can get right into it without getting pulled out of the story by distracting elements.

> "If there is shit all around me,
> how can I eat my ice cream?"
>
> —S. Balaram

Plus – you've already made the sale. You don't need to impress the readers with anything other than great content (as long as it's professional enough to give a great reading experience). Got it? Great – the following sections will deal with formatting in Word and InDesign more directly.

HOW TO FORMAT A BOOK IN MS WORD

I use MS Word 2010; unfortunately I'm not going to do a different guide for each version of Word but they should be mostly similar. If you aren't using MS Word, you'll find similar features in Open Office or other word processors.

GETTING STARTED

Open a new document. Click "size">> "More paper sizes" and set the document to 6"x9" (or your book size).

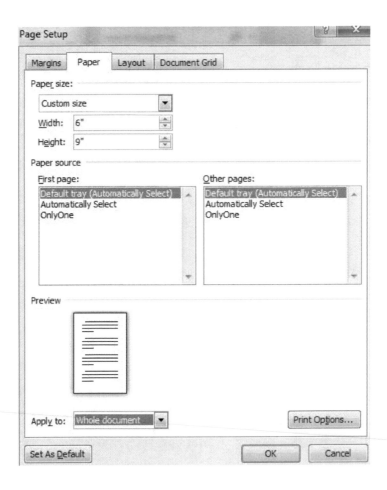

Then set the margins and gutter. Make sure to apply to the "whole document" instead of "this section."

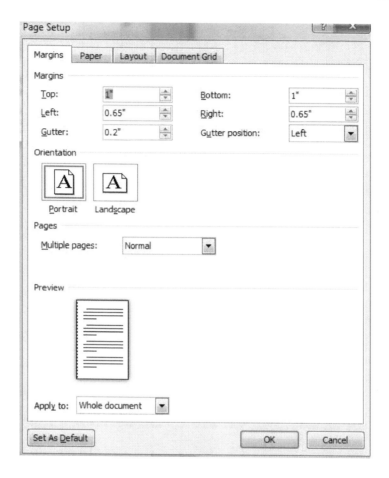

I set this one to 1" margins on the top and bottom (a bit too much on the top). The "Gutter" is extra space on the inside. Recently (2014) I've noticed that Createspace book spines are much more glued-together, so the gutter may need to be a little bigger.

Copy and paste your text into the document (or, if you've already been writing in Word, save the document as a new file (to be safe) and then start formatting.

SETTING PARAGRAPHS

Highlight some text and click on the "line options" tab.

Set the indent for the first line of paragraphs to .2 or so (I started with .3, but that's too much).

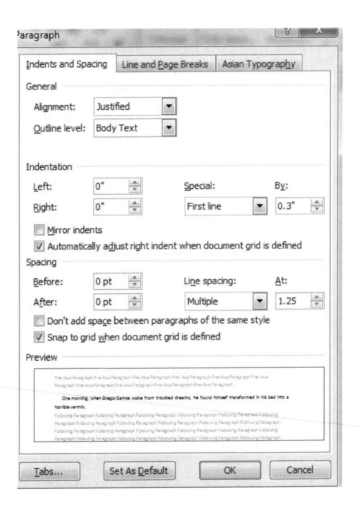

Make sure there's no space before or after the paragraph, and justified text. Select the font you want to use. With that text still selected, right click, go to "Styles" and "Update Normal to Match Selection."

Now your whole document is using the "Normal style."

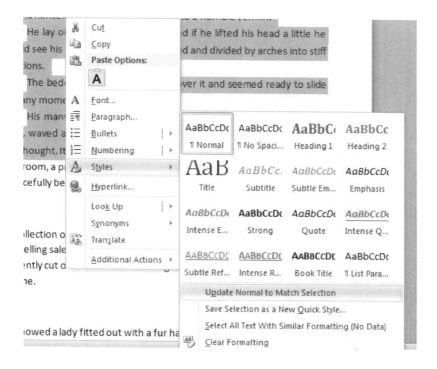

Then select the first paragraph of your book, click line spacing options again, but set the first line indent at 0.0. This time, right click and "Save the selection as a new style."

Save it as "First Paragraph."

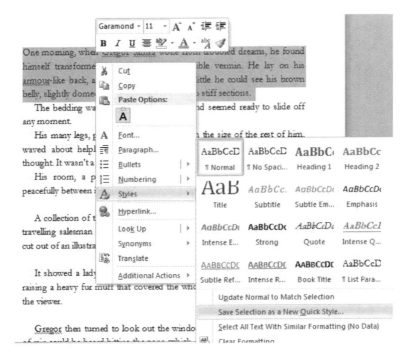

One morning, when Gregor Samsa woke from troubled dreams, he found himself transformed ... ble vermin. He lay on his armour-like back, a ... little he could see his brown belly, slightly domed ... o stiff sections.

The bedding wa ... d seemed ready to slide off any moment.

His many legs, ... the size of the rest of him. waved about helpl ... thought. It wasn't a ...

His room, a p ... peacefully between ...

A collection of t ... travelling salesman ... cut out of an illustra ...

It showed a lady ... raising a heavy fur muff that covered the who ... the viewer.

Gregor then turned to look out the windo ...

CHAPTER PAGES

Next, we're going to separate all the chapters.

This will be really important later when we start adding headers and footers.

So put the cursor before any of the text, go to "Page Layout" >> "Breaks" and "Next Page."

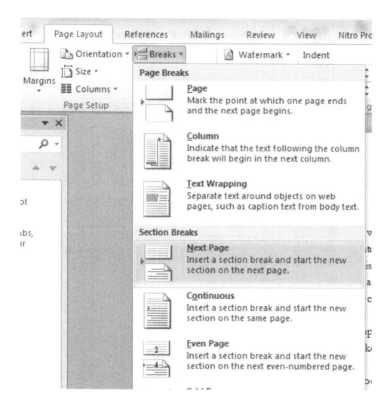

If you've done this right, the first page will say "First page Footer, Section 1" and the top of the next page will say "First Page Header, Section 2."

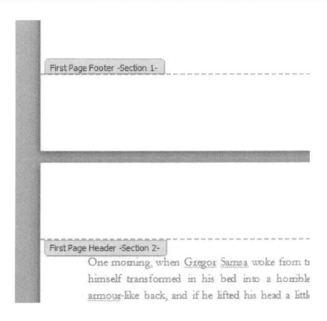

Click into the headers area (by clicking the space at the top of the page) and make sure you've checked "Different First Page" and "Different Odd and Even Pages."

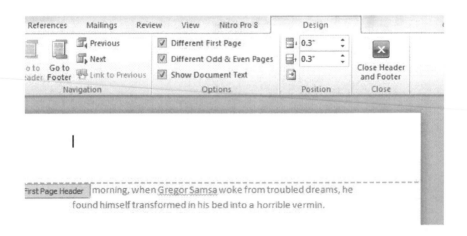

Because this is the first page of the first chapter, you can begin styling the chapter pages.

To make use of Word's built in Table of Contents function, it's best to start with Word's preset "Heading One."

Just type "Chapter One", select it, pick "Heading 1" from the styles, then change the size and font, select the text and right-click, then under "styles" click "Update Heading One to match selection."

I've changed the font to no-indent, black, and "Bebas Neue."

You may want to expand the text by bringing up the fonts menu (Ctrl+D on Windows) go to advanced, spacing and "expanded."

You should also check to make sure there's no indent on your chapter title, so that it's really centered.

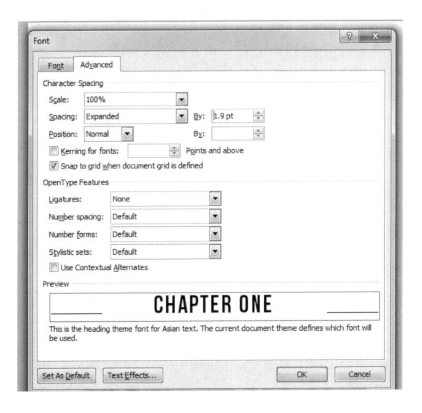

If you have a "Navigation" window open on the left side, this heading should show up right away.

Now you may want to style the first sentence. Select the first few words, and transform them to uppercase by going to the "Change Case" button on the Home menu.

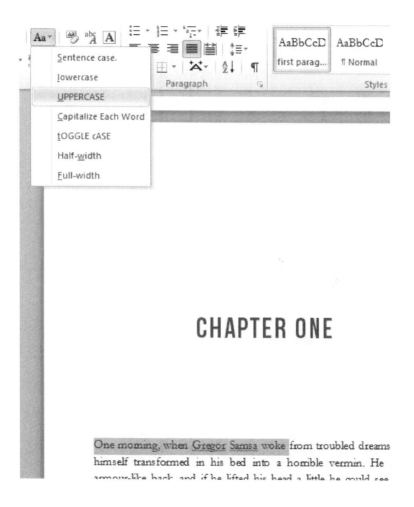

Then, to add a drop cap, put the cursor before the first letter of the first sentence, then go to the Insert panel and click the drop cap feature.

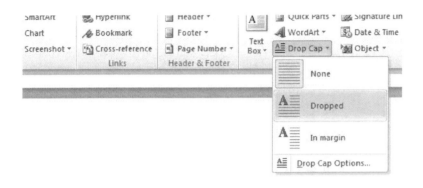

CHAPTER ONE

ONE MORNING, WHEN GREGOR SAMSA WOKE from troubled dreams, he found himself transformed in his bed into a horrible vermin. He lay on his armour-like back, and if he lifted

You can change the font of the Drop cap to stand out even more, but getting the positioning right can be tricky. If you want the Drop cap to take two lines instead of three, choose "Drop cap options" from the menu.

Now that our first page is ready, move down to the second page and click in the top area to select the header. Up on the menu, the "Link to Previous" is probably selected. You want to click on it to unlink it (just for the first pages, so they don't link with the front matter. For the remaining pages, you'll want link to previous selected).

I'll type in "Book Title", get the style right and then save it as a new quick style ("headers").

I'll align right. If you have "gutter" set up, you can see that the "inside" of the page (on the left) has more spacing. You want to align your headers and footers to the outside, so make sure it's on the side of the page with the smaller margins.

Then I'll go into the footers area, click "Insert", then page numbers>>current position>>plain number.

This enters a page number field.

Mine starts on page 3. If I want to change this, I could go to Insert>>page numbers>>Format page numbers and then choose "start at #…" instead of "continue from previous section."

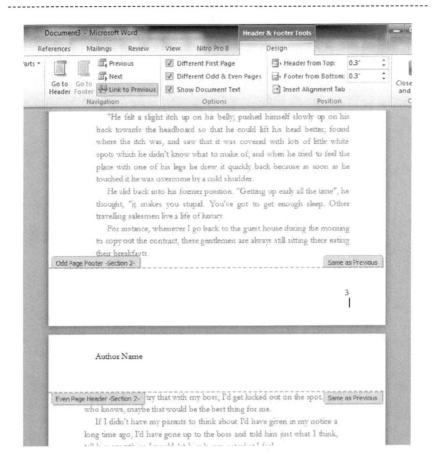

Then I can go down to the next page.

Because I've selected "Different Odd & Even Pages" I can make this page a little different, by aligning left and typing "Author Name." Then, instead of inserting the page number again, I can just select and copy the page number field from the previous page, and paste it into the footer of this page – aligning it left like the header.

To check my work, I'll go to "View" and hit the "Two pages" so I can make sure that it looks OK.

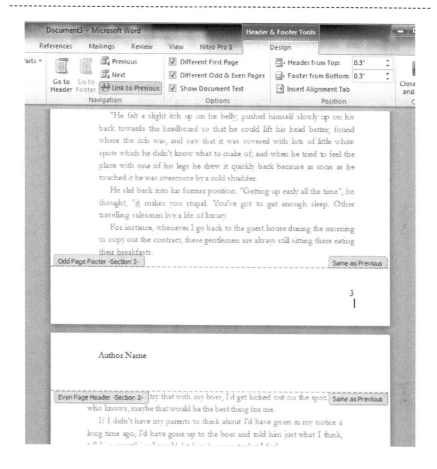

There's a little too much space between my headers and the content... but that's because I set my top page margins to 1" (a bit much). I'll leave it for now. The headings and page numbers look fine, so I'll go back to View>> 100% and continue on.

The whole first chapter should look pretty good now. If I want to style section breaks I could... a simple way is to use the "First Paragraph" style again with all caps on the first few words, but no Drop caps.

He'd fall right off his desk!

And it's a funny sort of business to be sitting up there at your talking down at your subordinates from up there, especially when you to go right up close because the boss is hard of hearing.

WELL, THERE'S STILL SOME HOPE; once I've got the money tog to pay off my parents' debt to him - another five or six years I supp that's definitely what I'll do. That's when I'll make the big change.

First of all though, I've got to get up, my train leaves at five. "As looked over at the alarm clock, ticking on the chest of drawers. "G Heaven!" he thought.

It was half past six and the hands were quietly moving forwards, i even later than half past, more like quarter to seven. Had the alarm not rung?

He could see from the bed that it had been set for four o'clock should have been; it certainly must have rung. Yes, but was it possil

When I get down to the bottom of the chapter, I'll put the cursor below the text, select Page layout>>Breaks >> and hit "Next Page" again.

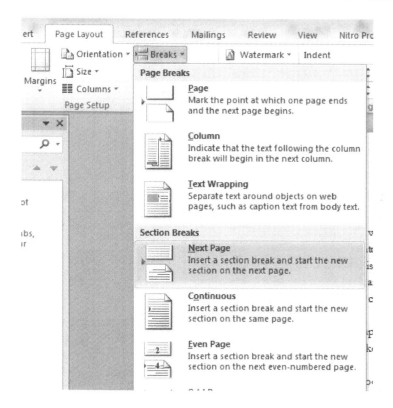

Because this is the first page of a new section, and we've selected "Different First Page" this page should be blank, with no headers and footers, so you can style it like the first Chapter Page.

In Word, it's hard to line up everything exactly. The best way to get it 100% consistent is to select and copy from just above the first paragraph to the top of the page, including all the spaces and Chapter Header, and then pasting it the first page of the next chapter. That's also a little faster than redoing everything manually. Then I can just change the text to "Chapter Two".

The following pages in the book should have the same headers and footers, and the page numbers should be automatic. So all you need to do is skip through and adding "Next Page" breaks between every chapter, and styling the chapter pages.

If your page numbers aren't working for any reason, make sure the "Link to Previous" option is selected.

If they still aren't connecting, go to format page numbers and "continue from previous."

You can also just select the page number field from the previous section and copy it into the one that's broken.

If you've been setting all your quick styles (first paragraph, normal, header, headings, page numbers) going through the chapters like this should be pretty fast.

If you get stuck with anything, it will probably be with the headings and footers and page numbers.

When you finish styling your chapters, switch to Two-Pages view so you can check everything over.

Right and left-align can be confusing, even if you are viewing it in Two-Pages mode, because Word may not show it as it actually prints.

Just keep in mind the extra wide margins are the inside gutter, so these are aligned on the outside, even though they look like they will be on the inside.

If you've been using the "Heading 1" style, Word has automatically been adding in your chapters to the navigation, which you should see on the navigation panel on the left.

So let's go back to the front and add the "front matter", including the table of contents.

ADDING THE COPYRIGHT PAGE, TITLE PAGE AND TOC

Put the cursor before chapter one and add a new "Next Page" break. You'll need these pages:

1. Title Page
2. Copyright page
3. Table of Contents
4. Dedication.

Your title page will want to match the cover pretty closely – see if your designer will give you the fonts he used – you may need to space out the lettering quite a bit. If you ask, your designer can probably save you a transparent PNG of the cover text (just like on the cover, but without the art) that you can add into the title page.

Your copyright page will look something like this (you can use this if you want):

TITLE Copyright © 2013 by Author Name.
All rights reserved. Printed in the United States of America. No part of this book may be used or reproduced in any manner whatsoever without written permission except in the case of brief quotations embodied in critical articles or reviews.
This book is a work of fiction. Names, characters, businesses, organizations, places, events and incidents either are the product of the author's imagination or are used fictitiously. Any resemblance to actual persons, living or dead, events, or locales is entirely coincidental.
For information contact; address www.website.com
Book and Cover design by Designer
ISBN: 123456789
First Edition: Month 2013
10 9 8 7 6 5 4 3 2 1

The "10 9 8 7 6 5 4 3 2 1" on the bottom refers to the editions, so if it goes until "1" it means first edition.

If this was the fourth edition, you'd write: "10 9 8 7 6 5 4".

These numbers should be close to the bottom of the page.

It can be centered, left or right aligned, and with much smaller font size (9 or 10).

If you're indie publishing, the copyright page isn't a big deal – in fact you can stand out by using something more creative. I tend to use a simple message like "Feel free to share this – just don't try to pass it off as your own! If you enjoy this book, I really hope you'll do me the favor of leaving a review. You can connect with me @ creativindie."

There's something to be said for trying to look as professional as possible though, especially with the print book; but I also think it's fine to "own up to" and even take pride in the fact that you self-published, as some skeptics may feel you're "trying to hide it" otherwise.

Ebooks, incidentally, will often skip past these front matter pages altogether. Amazon should do this automatically, setting the preview to start from the introduction or first chapter, and most Kindle books will do this as well (which is one reason why, if you want anybody to see it, you may want to put your front matter in the back of your ebooks).

Now make another "next page" break.

Then go to the "references" tab and hit Table of Contents.

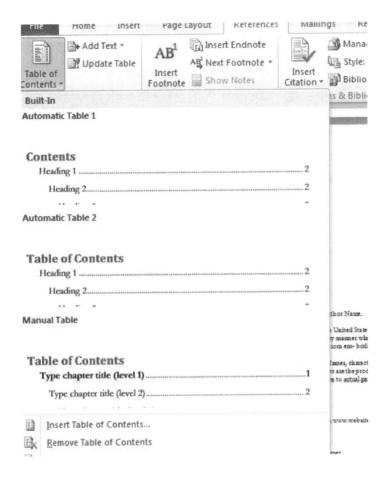

You should get an automatic Table of Contents. You may need to delete some areas, or change the fonts and styles (if you do, make sure to save it as a new style... it's really annoying to keep restyling it if you forget to do this).

Because this table is automatic, you can "Update Table" and "Update Page Numbers Only" if you do rewrites or add content later.

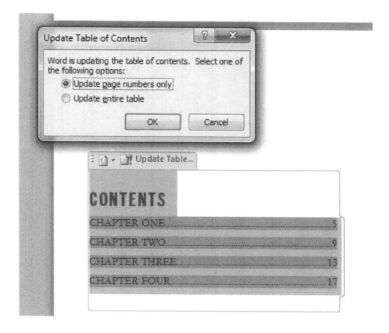

For the TOC, you probably need to make the text about 14pt, and add a little more spacing. If this is a novel, you don't really need a table of contents, but that's up to you.

For the front pages, you'll probably want to make sure there aren't any indents anywhere, so everything is properly aligned.

Be a little careful on these front pages – if a header or footer gets added in, and a later page is set to "link to previous" – then when you delete it on the front pages it will erase the headers and footers throughout the book. Instead, go to the next page with headers and uncheck "link to previous" – then you can delete the headers on the front pages.

Also, the copyright page is usually on the back of the title page (on the left hand side), while the dedication, Table of Contents and Chapter One usually starts on the right hand side – this means you'll have to leave some blank pages in between.

You can zoom way out to see everything together. Sometimes I need to use a real book, or picture the pages on my hand and flip my palm back and forth, to get this right.

Note – some books have all chapter pages on the right hand side – if you want to do that, just add an extra blank page by adding more "Next Page" breaks, and make sure they aren't connected to any headers or footers so they stay blank.

That's it – I'm going to attach the sample I made for this tutorial, you can download it by clicking these links:

Template-sample(.docx)

Template-sample (.doc)

They won't look the same unless you have the same fonts… so the first thing you'll want to do is change the Chapter Heading font to something that matches your book. Hopefully you've already got a great book cover, but if not, take a look at my list of best fonts per genre.

If you get stuck and are frustrated, find someone on Fiverr.com. Pay them $10 to $25 to fix whatever problem you're stuck on; it's worth it.

Ps) It can save some time if you learn a few useful keyboard shortcuts for MS Word. The one I use the most is "Ctrl+z" which undoes your last action.

FORMATTING A BOOK IN ADOBE INDESIGN

There are two main advantages to InDesign over Word. First, you have "Master Pages" – which lets you set document-wide options for your book. For example you can make one Master Page for the chapter pages – with no headers or footers – and another for the other pages, with headers and footers. Then, instead of having to manually add or remove those elements from every page, you can just assign a Master Page style to the special pages and you're done.

InDesign is also smarter about spacing text, so that the flow and spread of the letters and words is more even and harmonious. Word can sometimes get stuck and leave space gaps in the text.

Rather than starting from scratch, this guide to InDesign formatting will assume you're using one of my InDesign book templates. That way we'll skip a lot of technical stuff you don't really need to know about. Even so, InDesign can be frustratingly complex. I recommend hiring someone to do the initial formatting. If you have your book ready and send them the fonts and clear instructions (along with a template) it should cost less than $50.

I usually open up an InDesign template and format just the first few pages of the first chapter – styling the chapter headings, first paragraph and headings/footers, choosing the font and spacing and line-height. Then I'll send that to my formatter and let them finish the job, insert the front matter and Table of Contents.

But it's nice to have InDesign and know how to use it, so that I can later make small changes or fix typos without having to go back to my designer each time.

LET'S GET STARTED

I'm going to match the style with this cover I made for <u>www.diybookcovers.com</u>.

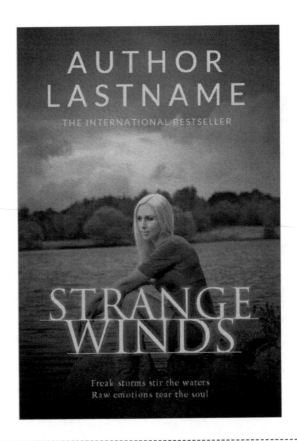

I'm going to start with a very simple, basic InDesign Book Template. Here's the link to the template I'm using in case you're following along: IndesignbooktemplateNEW.indd

The first thing I'm going to do is copy the first chapter of my book (from the Word file, or wherever you have it), and paste it into the first paragraph of the InDesign file.

Pages should automatically be added, so that the rest of the text is pushed down to the end of the document. (If that doesn't happen, I'll tell you how to fix it later.)

For now let's set up our main styles.

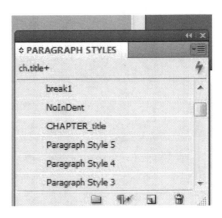

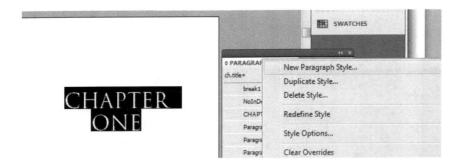

I'll highlight the "Chapter One" text and set it to Trajan Pro, all caps to match the cover. Then I'll highlight the text again, and hit the little panel button on the top right of the Paragraph Styles panel (right under the X to close the panel). I'm going to save this as a "new paragraph style" rename it "Header1."

Now "Header1" shows up under my Paragraph Styles – next time I get to a chapter heading, I'll just highlight it and hit that style. If I want to edit the style for all chapter headings, I'll click on the style in the Paragraph Styles panel and adjust things (for example, I'll probably want the letters to be spaced out a bit, so I can go to "basic character formats" and increase the "tracking.")

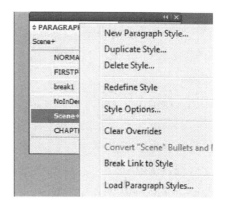

I'll do the same thing for the subtitle, increasing the font size, making sure the text is centered. I change the font to "Lato" to match the cover, then save it as "Scene" (because in this book, the subtitles describe the scene). If I make changes to the text on the page, I can highlight it, hit the little box inside the Paragraph Styles panel again and choose "Redefine Style" so that my changes are automatically applied to the style.

For the first paragraph, I'm going to set the font to Sabon, 11pt, with 18pt line spacing. Then I'll save it as a new style, "NoIndent." Next, I'll open that style and adjust the "Indents and spacing" so there's actually no indent. I do the same for the next paragraph, but setting an indent, and saving it as "Normal." (When you pasted your text in, it probably already had a style assigned by default. You can just redefine the current style so it applies to most of your text. Or, set the second paragraph style first, and then paste your text into that paragraph to keep the style.)

I wasn't quite happy so I fiddled some more, making the subtitle smaller. Then I added a Drop cap, by going to the little extra panel at the very right of the top menu, which gives me a Drop cap option.

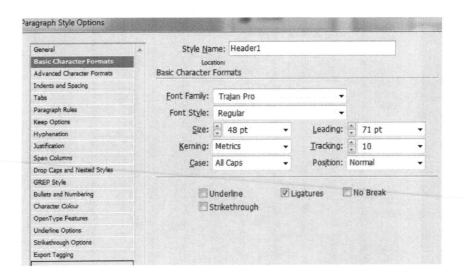

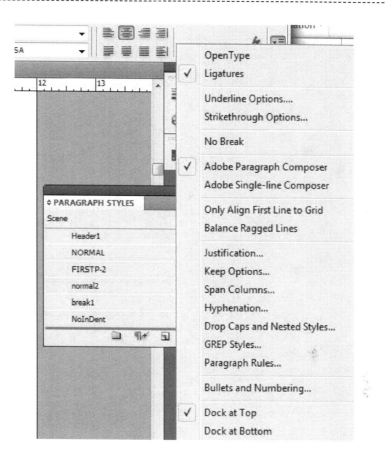

Then I selected the first few words of the first sentence and made them all-caps.

This is what my first page looks like now.

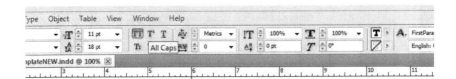

CHAPTER
ONE

Arrest - Conversation with Mrs. Grubach - Then Miss Bürstner

SOMEONE MUST HAVE BEEN TELLING LIES about Josef K., he knew he had done nothing wrong but, one morning, he was arrested.
Every day at eight in the morning he was brought his breakfast by Mrs. Grubach's cook - Mrs. Grubach was his landlady - but to-

USING MASTER PAGES

If I scroll down to the next page, I can see that everything looks pretty good, except that I need to adjust my headers. You can't just click up in that area to edit them however; that information is set on a "Master Page."

with many folds and pockets, buckles and buttons and a belt, all of which gave the impression of being very practical but without making it very clear what they were actually for.

"Who are you?" asked K., sitting half upright in his bed.

The man, however, ignored the question as if his arrival simply had to be accepted, and merely replied, "You rang?"

"Anna should have brought me my breakfast," said K.

He tried to work out who the man actually was, first in silence, just through observation and by thinking about it, but the man didn't stay still to be looked at for very long.

Instead he went over to the door, opened it slightly, and said to someone who was clearly standing immediately behind it, "He wants Anna to bring him his breakfast."

There was a little laughter in the neighbouring room, it was not clear from the sound of it whether there were several people laughing.

The strange man could not have learned anything from it that he hadn't known already, but now he said to K. as if making his report "It is not possible."

"It would be the first time that's happened," said K., as he jumped out of bed and quickly pulled on his trousers.

"I want to see who that is in the next room, and why it is that Mrs. Grubach has let me be disturbed in this way."

It immediately occurred to him that he needn't have said this out

"I meant it for your own good," said the stranger and opened the door, this time without being asked.

The next room, which K. entered more slowly than he had intended, looked at first glance exactly the same as it had the previous evening.

It was Mrs. Grubach's living room, over-filled with furniture, table-cloths, porcelain and photographs.

Perhaps there was a little more space in there than usual today, but if so it was not immediately obvious, especially as the main difference was the presence of a man sitting by the open window with a book from which he now looked up.

"You should have stayed in your room!

Didn't Franz tell you?"

"And what is it you want, then?" said K., looking back and forth between this new acquaintance and the one named Franz, who had remained in the doorway.

Through the open window he noticed the old woman again, who had come close to the window opposite so that she could continue to see everything.

She was showing an inquisitiveness that really made it seem like she was going senile. "I want to see Mrs. Grubach . . .," said K., making a movement as if tearing himself away from the two men - even though they were standing well away from him - and wanted to go.

"No," said the man at the window, who threw his book down on a

If I click on the Pages Panel, in the main box I can see my document and all the pages – in those little icons, at the top, is an "H" or an "I". Those are two different master page styles. At the top of that panel are my master pages, called "H" and "I".

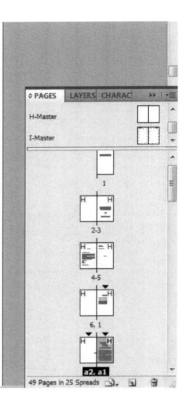

BOOK TITLE | 3

t it for your own good," said the stranger and opened the door,
ithout being asked.

t room, which K. entered more slowly than he had intended,
rst glance exactly the same as it had the previous evening.

frs. Grubach's living room, over-filled with furniture, table-
:elain and photographs.

there was a little more space in there than usual today, but
not immediately obvious, especially as the main difference
sence of a man sitting by the open window with a book from
ɔw looked up.

ould have stayed in your room!

'ranz tell you?"

hat is it you want, then?" said K., looking back and forth
is new acquaintance and the one named Franz, who had re-
he doorway.

ı the open window he noticed the old woman again, who had
: to the window opposite so that she could continue to see

showing an inquisitiveness that really made it seem like she
senile. "I want to see Mrs. Grubach ... ," said K., making a
as if tearing himself away from the two men - even though
tanding well away from him - and wanted to go.

ıid the man at the window, who threw his book down on a
: and stood up.

"H" is totally blank, with no headers, for my chapter pages or
front matter. "I" has headings and page numbers. If I click on that
template, I can change the author name and book name, and style
it a bit.

The Trial | 1

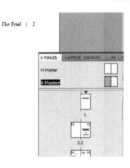

I don't want to do anything with the page numbers, which display here as only the symbol "I" (if this is confusing, my master pages could have been named "A" or "B" or something else. It's just in this template I started with, they are called "H" and "I".)

Those page numbers are automatic, so on this page there's just a placeholder symbol.

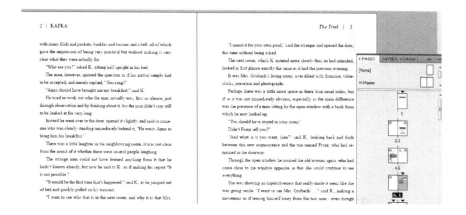

If I click back in the document section of the pages panel I can see that my changes are kept.

Next I'll scroll all the way down to the end of Chapter One, doing a quick check. Something I notice is that several pages are blank and don't have headers. That's because, in the original template, these pages were set with the master page "H."

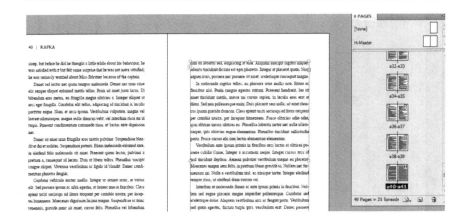

I need to reset them with the master page style "I".

In the Pages Panel, I put my mouse over the page I want to change and right click, then choose "Apply Master to Pages." Then I'll pick the style I want.

Since my original template had short chapters, now that I've put in my text I need to do this several times.

OVERSET TEXT

When I get down the end of the document, I notice a lot of the text is cut off.

My template was only for 49 pages, and when I added my new text InDesign didn't make new pages for me. If I click the arrow tool from the tools panel, and then click in the text area of the page, it will show me a red "+" sign – that means there's overset text.

metus justo in mi.

t tortor a pretium. Sed quis imperdiet enim, nus tincidunt, ante nec aliquam mollis, justo t eleifend nisl nisl mattis justo. Proin at enim drerit tincidunt nec magna. Ut nec orci at nis

First, I'm going to insert some more pages. I right click on that last page (in the Pages Panel) and choose "insert pages." I'm going to add 50 for now.

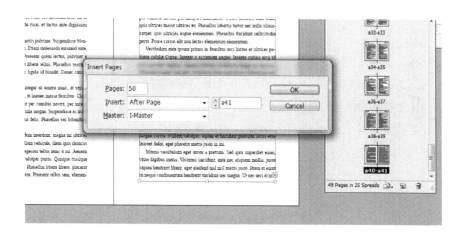

Then, I'll go back and click on that little red "+" sign. Now there will be a little snippet or preview of the text under my mouse; I'll go down to the next blank page of the new pages I made, and click the mouse again.

All the overset text will be copied in.

This will work fine as long as you made enough pages for the overset text. But if you didn't, on the last page you'll get that red "+" sign again.

But there's a way to avoid this if you aren't sure. After hitting the red "+" and getting the overset text on your mouse, hold down shift when you click in to the next page. Now under the mouse, instead of the text you'll see a little snaky line – that means you have the "autoflow" feature on.

If you click the mouse while holding shift this way, when you paste the text InDesign will automatically add extra pages as needed.

So now I've pasted the rest of my book, but I still need to go through it and apply the styles to all the chapter pages; and also apply the right master page to those pages (and remove it from any that should be 'normal' pages with the header and footer).

A quick cheat is to go back and highlight the first paragraph and heading from the first chapter, and copy+paste it to the first pages of other chapters. Then I just have to change all the text to make it right. For me, that's faster than selecting the right style for each element, redoing the Drop cap, etc.

UPDATING THE TABLE OF CONTENTS

My templates should have a TOC already, but you'll need to update it. Go up to the Layout tab and you'll find the Table of Contents menu.

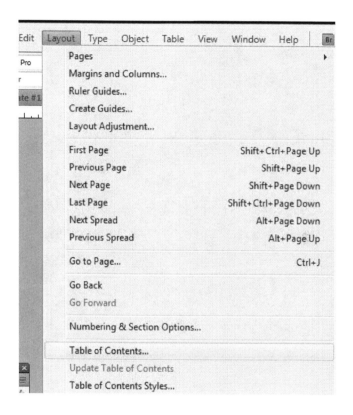

I used "Header1" for the chapter titles, so I need to add that style to the TOC instead of the default ones.

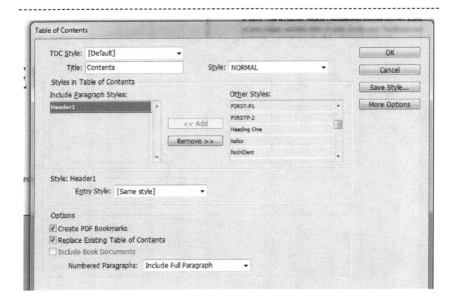

That sort of worked, except it divided up the Header1 tags into two entries, so I'll need to combine them all, and add some styling.

Contents

Chapter   1

One   1

Chapter   43

TWO   43

Chapter   52

THREE   52

Chapter   61

FOUR 61

EPILOGUE   70

If you need more help, I recommend searching YouTube for your specific problem, "How to X in InDesign?" or signing up with Lynda. com for some more robust training.

As I said earlier though, rather than beating your head against a wall, I'd give it to someone on Fiverr.com and pay to have it done well, and right (otherwise, what's the point of using InDesign?)

HOW TO MAKE AN EBOOK
(KINDLE, EPUB AND SMASHWORDS)

No matter what kind of book you're publishing, ebook sales will probably be your biggest numbers. Since ebooks have no production costs, they let you be much more flexible in pricing, and can be a powerful marketing tool to attract new readers.

So even while you're formatting for print, you should be thinking about ebook conversion. Luckily, you can do it for free, and it can be pretty easy – if you aren't picky about the little details (and I'll explain why you shouldn't be).

Below you'll find a few different methods for converting your document to epub and mobi formats, as well as formatting a Smashwords file (ideal for broader distribution).

TERMINOLOGY CRASH COURSE

"Ebooks" are digital versions of your book that can be read on tablets and smartphones. Most ebook stores use a file format called "epub" – but Amazon/Kindle uses a slightly modified file format called "mobi." Most bookstore chains have their own ereader device and their own bookstore; but some companies like Smashwords, BookBaby, and Lulu offer "distribution" – which means they'll send your ebook out to all the online retailers and keep track of sales for you.

GETTING STARTED

Unlike print books, for which you want everything to be "fixed" and perfect, ebooks need to "flow."

This is so people using various ereaders can set their own options, change the fonts and text size, to make the reading experience suit their preferences. To achieve this, ebook formats use something very similar to html code. While you don't really need to learn this code, it will help if you need to fine tune the details.

When I first started learning ebook formatting, it was frustrating. I was trying to approach it like a print book, and insert images and special designs, and fixed fonts. While this can be done, my complex code would look fine on Kindle or Barnes & Noble but might like strange on Kobo.

It's very hard to get your file to look exactly the same everywhere. The most important thing is that – even if it doesn't look the same – it doesn't look "broken" or obviously flawed.

For this reason, most mainstream publishers use extremely simple ebooks with no decoration at all. Even if you try to use a Drop cap or special formatting, it might look funny. So don't get hung up on the small details. Keep it simple.

WHAT YOU CAN DO

Basically, you'll use "H1" or "H2" tags for headers. Your text will be justified. The first paragraphs of each chapter will be non-indented. And maybe you'll offset the first line in all caps, or a slightly bolded or larger first sentence.

I'm taking a picture of a bunch of the books on my Kindle so you can get a sense of what they look like.

CHAPTER TWO

JESSICA

The rain pounded the pavement, causing steam to rise from its black surface. It drove in a lot of people who normally might not have come into the bookstore. The flash storm had caught everyone by surprise; no one expected it since the sky had been blue and sunny just a half hour before.

I watched people from the register, eying their movements, watching the way they interacted with things, other people. They seemed so different from myself now. They were so normal. They chatted and laughed with their friends. They picked up books, glanced over them, set them back down. They went about their every day lives like there was nothing that existed outside of the norm. They knew nothing of angels, death, fear. I felt like a stranger in the human race, like I didn't belong here at all.

I envied them.

And yet I could never regret the events that had happened in my life. They had brought more love and

CHAPTER THREE
DETERMINE YOUR DESTINATION

A Brand-New Approach to Artist Branding

YOU, A BRAND? YES. REMEMBER, YOU ARE THE PRODUCT. YOU MUST FIND A WAY to build YOU into a brand. You must find a way to stand out in an increasingly noisy marketplace. You must connect emotionally with your audience. You must be seen as a cluster of positive perceptions.

There are so many writing and speaking brands that are unable to get off the ground because they are focused solely on their lives, their trauma, their testimony—with no regard for mentioning *why* their stories have anything to do with the audience! If people have never heard of you, they simply won't care about your story—unless you explain what's in it for them.

CHAPTER ONE

I wake with his name in my mouth.

Will.

Before I open my eyes, I watch him crumple to the pavement again. Dead.

My doing.

Tobias crouches in front of me, his hand on my left shoulder. The train car bumps over the rails, and Marcus, Peter, and Caleb stand by the doorway. I take a deep breath and hold it in an attempt to relieve some of the pressure that is building in my chest.

An hour ago, nothing that happened felt real to me. Now it does.

I breathe out, and the pressure is still there.

"Tris, come on," Tobias says, his eyes searching mine. "We have to jump."

PRESSIA

BOATS

THEY STEP INTO THE FRONT HALL—the chair rails, white walls, the flowered runner, and wide stairs leading to the second floor. It floods Pressia with a sharp sense of being penned, trapped. She still holds the bottle to her head, her fingers stiff, her entire body aching. She looks into the dining room; again she's startled by the brilliance of the chandelier trembling over the long table. She hears footsteps overhead— Ingership's wife? The chandelier makes Pressia think of her grandfather, the picture of him in the hospital bed. She tries to remember that feeling of hopefulness, but then recalls the dinner knife in her hand, the latex gloves, the burning in her stomach,

2. IT DOESN'T INTERRUPT

The Keebler Elves, the Trix bunny, the Yoplait ladies one-upping each other with ecstatic proclamations of how good the yogurt is—they were all created to entertain, so that the next time you were in the mood for cereal or a snack, you'd remember the funny ad and be compelled to try the product. The Marlboro Man's steely jaw and far-off stare were designed to convince you that if you smoked his cigarette, you too might exude an ounce of his masculine, independent essence. Ads and marketing are supposed to make consumers feel something and then act on that feeling. In that regard, the content marketers create today is similar

---

1

Know Your Numbers

Budgeting

Sowing on the good soil

Financial success and success in business are all about sowing seeds on the good soil. If we want to know where the good soil is, before we get started in Real Estate, it is important to know our numbers. I have noticed that many seasoned salespeople have no grasp of their personal finances, or the numbers of the sales business.

How much would you and your sales career benefit, if you

PART ONE

The Connection Economy Demands That We Create Art

Opportunities Amid the Junk

Just outside Harvard Square, at 29 Oxford Street, lies the Cruft Lab. Part of the physics department at Harvard, this is where George Washington Pierce invented the crystal oscillator about a hundred years ago. Without his invention, radio stations would never have been commercially feasible.

But Cruft Hall is even more important for giving its name to a vitally important concept. "Cruft" is the engineering term for the leftover detritus, useless

EIGHTEEN

THE REST OF the words lay on my tongue, unspoken. I hugged myself, closing my eyes. Grief was already seeping into my veins, but I couldn't process anything I was feeling yet.

"It gets easier," Adam said. His voice was surprisingly gentle.

I opened my eyes and looked at him. He stood a few feet away, his hand on the panel that had made the gate spring to life, his hair blowing in the wind. Abel stood beside him. They looked so alike, and I was struck by the nobleness in their eyes as they drew back a few paces, giving me space to feel my sorrow.

After another moment of breathing in and out, I straightened and approached them. I might be head over heels for a boy, something I'd never foreseen happening to me, but I hadn't turned wholly stupid. It was dangerous here.

"We should go," I said, and he nodded.

2
Stop Brainstorming and Take a Shower

A person with a new idea is a crank until the idea succeeds.
—MARK TWAIN

A Mind of Your Own

Eleven men and women file into a conference room and take their places around a large table. Coffee cups and pastries are assembled in front of them. George, the leader, steps up to a large whiteboard and scrawls across the top "SOAP STORM SESSION 9/18/12." "Okay, let's begin," he tells the group. "Let's just start free-associating. What do we

> ## Epilogue
> ### THE ASCENT BECKONS
>
> The hospital hallway was blindingly white. After so many days living by torchlight, gaslight, and eerie witchlight, the fluorescent lighting made things look sallow and unnatural. When Clary signed herself in at the front desk, she noticed that the nurse handing her the clipboard had skin that looked strangely yellowish under the bright lights. *Maybe she's a demon,* Clary thought, handing the clipboard back. "Last door at the end of the hall," said the nurse, flashing a kind smile. *Or I could be going crazy.*
>
> "I know," said Clary. "I was here yesterday." *And the day before, and the day before that.* It was early evening, and the hallway wasn't crowded. An old

These books are mainstream bestsellers. If you're like me, you're probably thinking these don't look very good. And that may seem depressing, but it should be liberating: you don't need to spend a lot of time or energy making your ebooks perfect, just make sure they work and are clean, and people can read your book without distraction.

If your book is in an MS Word file, you should actually have saved a simple copy before you did any print formatting. That's because your book file needs to be pretty simple to convert it to ebook. I'm going to use Kafka's The Trial for this tutorial.

If you used Scrivener or Adobe InDesign you can export as an Epub file directly; if you used another open source word processor you can probably save as RTF or HTML. In either case, skip down to the lower sections, like using Calibre or Sigil.

Hopefully you've been using the "Header 1" tag for all your Chapter Titles – so you should already have a "Navigation Panel" showing up with your chapters.

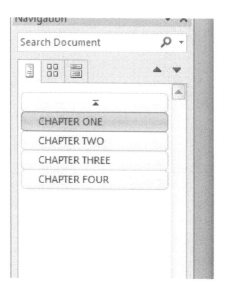

You may need to get rid of some troublesome features; you can use the Search and Replace feature to do so.

I usually search for double spaces and change them to single space, in case I've missed any.

You'll need to search for any "Tabs" and remove them: search for "^t" and just leave the "replace with" box empty. Your paragraphs should be indented with the "line space options" – if not, you can set the indent and then "update normal to match style".

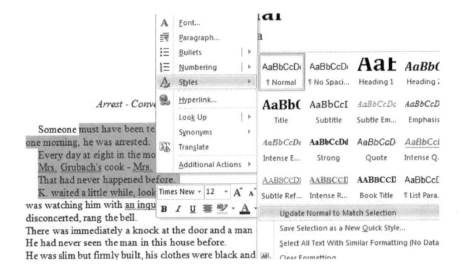

Your first line of new sections should already be using a non-indent style (different from "normal").

You should have added a new page break between sections. And if you have any images, you'll probably need to add them in later. This is what my Word file looks like:

Chapter One

Arrest - Conversation with Mrs. Grubach - Then Miss Bürstner

Someone must have been telling lies about Josef K., he knew he had done nothing wrong but, one morning, he was arrested.

Every day at eight in the morning he was brought his breakfast by Mrs. Grubach's cook - Mrs. Grubach was his landlady - but today she didn't come. That had never happened before.

K. waited a little while, looked from his pillow at the old woman who lived opposite and who was watching him with an inquisitiveness quite unusual for her, and finally, both hungry and disconcerted, rang the bell.

There was immediately a knock at the door and a man entered.

He had never seen the man in this house before.

He was slim but firmly built, his clothes were black and close-fitting, with many folds and pockets, buckles and buttons and a belt, all of which gave the impression of being very practical but without making it very clear what they were actually for.

"Who are you?" asked K., sitting half upright in his bed.

The man, however, ignored the question as if his arrival simply had to be accepted, and merely replied, "You rang?"

"Anna should have brought me my breakfast," said K.

I think it's pretty clean and simple, so I'm going to try and use an automatic converter first.

I've set up a simple conversion tool on my book covers site that you can use to test things quickly. Click on this link to try it out: http://bookcovers.creativindie.com/instant-online-ebook-conversion-to-epub/

You might want to save your document as HTML or RTF, but DOCX should work.

On that page you'll see this form.

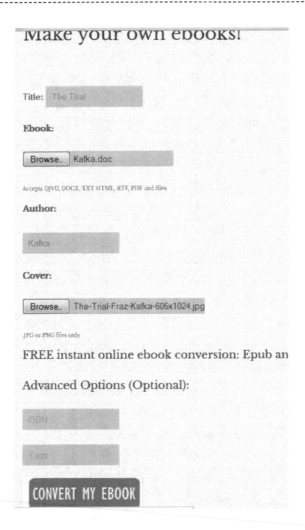

I uploaded my data, hit the button, and got these two links.

The mobi file wouldn't open with my Kindle application for some reason (I'm getting it checked). But the epub version looks great! I'm viewing it with Adobe Digital Previewer. The chapter heading style, italics, centering and non-indent on the first paragraph all came through fine.

Chapter One

Arrest - Conversation with Mrs. Grubach - Then Miss Bürstner

Someone must have been telling lies about Josef K., he knew he had done nothing wrong but, one morning, he was arrested.

Every day at eight in the morning he was brought his breakfast by Mrs. Grubach's cook - Mrs. Grubach was his landlady - but today she didn't come.

That had never happened before.

K. waited a little while, looked from his pillow at the old woman who lived opposite and who was watching him with an inquisitiveness quite unusual for her, and finally, both hungry and disconcerted, rang the bell.

There was immediately a knock at the door and a man entered.

He had never seen the man in this house before.

He was slim but firmly built, his clothes were black and close-fitting, with many folds and pockets, buckles and buttons and a belt, all of which gave the impression of being very practical but without making it very clear what they were actually for.

"Who are you?" asked K., sitting half upright in his bed.

The man, however, ignored the question as if his arrival simply had to be accepted, and merely replied, "You rang?"

"Anna should have brought me my breakfast," said K.

He tried to work out who the man actually was, first in silence, just through observation and by thinking about it, but the man didn't stay still to be looked at for very long.

Instead he went over to the door, opened it slightly, and said to someone who was clearly standing immediately behind it, "He wants Anna to bring him his breakfast."

Luckily there's a very simple trick for making Mobi files from the epub. Download the Kindle Previewer application for desktop: http://www.amazon.com/gp/feature.html?docId=1000765261

Then just drag and drop your epub file into the program – it will automatically convert to mobi and save the new file in the same folder that your epub was in.

If this worked for you, congrats, you're done!

Upload your files to Kindle, or preview them with as many previewer tools as you can to make sure they look OK.

MAKING AN EBOOK IN CALIBRE

If you want to go a little deeper into the process, you can download and install Calibre, which is free and pretty easy to use (although there's still some learning curve). This is what the program looks like.

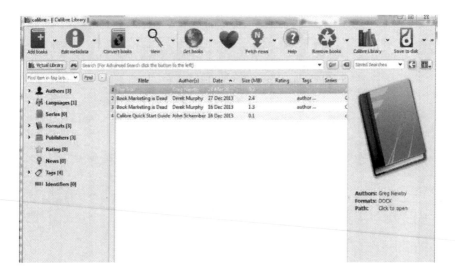

First I'll click on "Add Book" from the top left corner and choose my file. Then I'll click "Edit Metadata" to change the details and add my cover.

Then I'll click on "Convert Books." In this panel, on the top right where it says "Output Format" I can choose to output as Kindle,

Epub or another format (you need to do it one by one). On the left menu there are some more options, such as "Look and Feel."

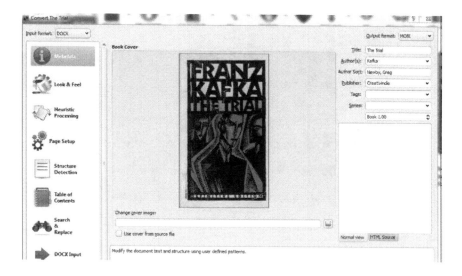

If my simple converter didn't work and you need to fix something (removing spacing between paragraphs for example) you may be able to do it here.

When you're ready, hit the green checkmark ("OK") on the bottom. It will think for a while, and then the new format will show up on the right side. Do this for mobi and epub (or just epub and use the Kindle Previewer trick), then click "Save to Disk" and choose where you want to save it.

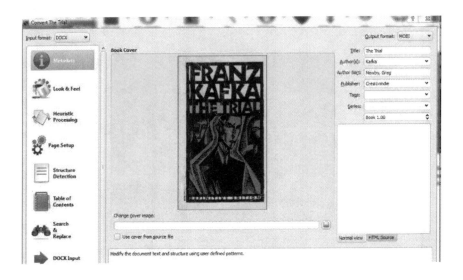

ADVANCED OPTIONS: USING SIGIL FOR FINE-TUNING

A lot of ebook formatters may take issue at my first two suggestions – they aren't the best way to make ebooks and the code may not be super clean. But for Kindle and the majority of ebook viewers, the files will work just fine. Plus, simple is better.

But if you want to learn to "do it right" – or you need to troubleshoot your ebook file (for example, you caught a typo you need to fix) Sigil is your best bet.

Also a free program (https://code.google.com/p/sigil/) Sigil lets you open up epub files and make changes. It only works for epub, so you'll need to save your epub and remake a new mobi file later.

I opened Sigil, went to "File" and "Open" and chose the epub file I made from my website.

The first page is the cover – and it may seem stretched because it will automatically adjust to the screen width. This is what Sigil looks like.

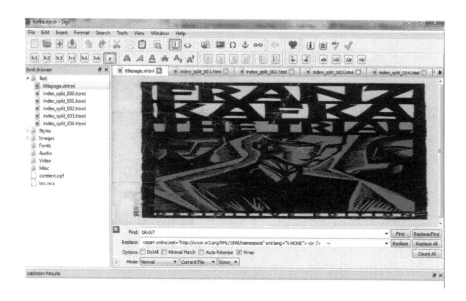

Each "section" is saved as its own unique html file – you can see them in the menu on the left. So I need to click on them until I get to the one I want to edit.

I can edit, add, erase anything in the text just like a normal word processor. I can also add bold, italics and basic formatting from the top menu. It even has a "find and replace" feature which can be really helpful if you want to change all instances of something (like you changed the name of your character from Bill to Tom).

To make simple changes, Sigil is worth getting to know, so you don't have to keep going back to a coder or formatter. If something is displaying strangely, you can hit the "code" view button (next to the "Book View" which is the default). Then you'll see the code, but be careful about changing things if you don't know what you're doing.

Your Chapter Headings should still be using the 'h1' style. If everything else looks OK, you can hit "Tools" and check that your cover, metadata (details about the book) and Table of Contents are right (clicking "Generate Table of Contents" will add all the header tags, but you can uncheck any extra ones that shouldn't be there).

Then you can resave the epub, and use the Kindle Previewer to convert it to mobi.

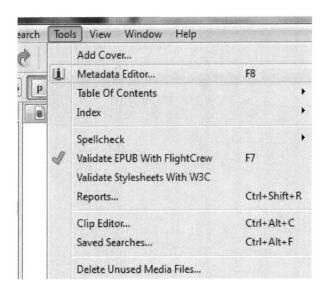

NOW LET'S TRY SOME FANCY STUFF.

Although simple is better, let's add some style for fun.

My "Chapter One" is using the "h1" tag (which translated all the way through from my Word document – that's why we use the "Heading 1" style.)

If I click on "styles" on the left, I can see the stylesheet – that's an external document that tells the html what it should look like. Right now that stylesheet is very simple, but I can add to it.

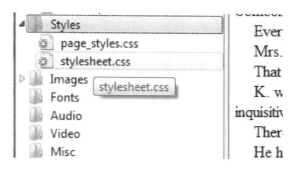

Let's change the font of the chapter headings. First, we need to import the font. Hit the "+" button on the top left, navigate to your fonts folder, and select a font (you could also copy and paste your font into the same folder your ebook files are in).

I chose Stag – but I'm not sure if I want light or bold, so I added both. The fonts will show up in the fonts folder.

Now go to the stylesheet. At the very top, before any other code, you need to add:

```
@font-face {
font-family:'Stag-light';
src: url(../Fonts/STAG-LIGHT_0.OTF);
}
```

That "src" needs to be the exact link to your font, so it has to match the font name on the left exactly.

If you want to simplify it, you can right click over the font and "rename" it to something simple.

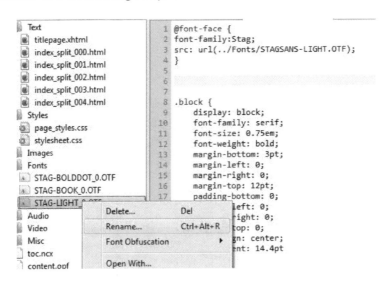

Now that I've added that to the top of my stylesheet, I can go down to the bottom and add new instructions for the H1 tags.

h1 {

font-family: 'Stag-light', serif;

}

The name of the font here needs to be exactly the same as above.

At first this wasn't working for me, so I went in and checked the code. Instead of clean H1 tags there was some other code (the dangers of using Calibre, which doesn't use clean tags). So I removed it and just used:

<h1>CHAPTER ONE</h1>

Now the font is showing up.

I used the buttons on the top right to change the text to all uppercase.

Now let's play with the first paragraph style.

I highlighted the first sentence and hit the uppercase button. But that looked a little too busy.

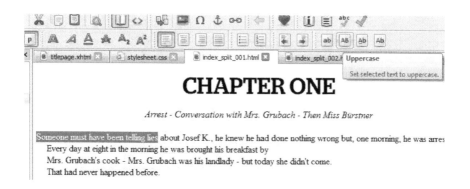

Instead I'm going to be content with just changing my subtitle to "h3" to make it stand out a bit more.

CHAPTER ONE

Arrest - Conversation with Mrs. Grubach - Then Miss Bürstner

Someone Must Have Been Telling Lies about Josef K., he knew he had done nothing wrong but, one morning, he was arreste
Every day at eight in the morning he was brought his breakfast by
Mrs. Grubach's cook - Mrs. Grubach was his landlady - but today she didn't come.
That had never happened before.
K. waited a little while, looked from his pillow at the old woman who lived opposite and who was watching him with an inquisitiveness quite unusual for her, and finally, both hungry and disconcerted, rang the bell.
There was immediately a knock at the door and a man entered.
He had never seen the man in this house before.
He was slim but firmly built, his clothes were black and close-fitting, with many folds and pockets, buckles and buttons and belt, all of which gave the impression of being very practical but without making it very clear what they were actually for.
"Who are you?" asked K., sitting half upright in his bed.

And just for fun, I'll add some decoration – first I hit the "+" button and choose a picture. This just adds the picture to the program but doesn't put it in the book; I need to hit "insert" and "file" to choose the picture I've just added. Then I can center and adjust it.

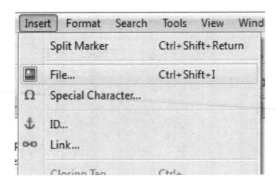

What I can't do easily is change the size of the picture.

In this one, there is too much white space around the graphic but I can't trim that off in Sigil, I'd need to crop it in an image viewer or graphics program, save it, and try again.

CHAPTER ONE

Arrest - Conversation with Mrs. Grubach - Then Miss
Bürstner

Someone Must Have Been Telling Lies about Josef K., he knew he had
done nothing wrong but, one morning, he was arrested.

Every day at eight in the morning he was brought his breakfast by
Mrs. Grubach's cook - Mrs. Grubach was his landlady - but today she
didn't come.

That had never happened before.

K. waited a little while, looked from his pillow at the old woman who
lived opposite and who was watching him with an inquisitiveness quite
unusual for her, and finally, both hungry and disconcerted, rang the bell.

There was immediately a knock at the door and a man entered.

He had never seen the man in this house before.

He was slim but firmly built, his clothes were black and close-fitting, wit

One thing to notice: my computer screen is pretty wide, but
if I make the window more narrow (like most ebook readers) my
subtitle breaks into two lines. This is annoying, but common – the
only way to fix it would be to make the text smaller. If you test it on
some ebook readers and it always breaks, you could try a smaller
size. Perhaps just bold italics and not a header tag.

But if it only happens on a few, don't stress it too much.

The main thing is to get things right in the Word document,
rather than messing around with things too much in Sigil.

EVEN MORE ADVANCED (THE 'RIGHT' WAY)

Another way to make ebooks (more professional, but more time-consuming) is to copy all the text from your Word document and use an online service like "word2cleanhtml.com" to make it cleaner.

Then, open a new document in Sigil and paste all that html code in between the body tags.

```
 3      "http://www.w3.org/TR/xhtml11/DTD/xhtml11.dtd">
 4
 5  <html xmlns="http://www.w3.org/1999/xhtml">
 6  <head>
 7  <title></title>
 8  </head>
 9  <body>
10  <p> </p>
11  </body>
12  </html>
```

That's the safest way to do it – manually coding the whole book. It doesn't take that long; you just need to skip down to end of each chapter, hit "split at cursor" under the "edit" menu, highlight all the chapter headings and select H1, add your style to the first paragraph (although – coding the "no indent" first paragraph is a little tricky... You'd need to make two styles in the style sheet; one for normal text, one for no indent.)

Once you get used to it, it's quick. But it's still a pain, and so I either use my free ebook generator, or I hire someone on Fiverr. com to convert to ebook files for me, because there's really no need to add style, and it can actually sabotage the process.

The average price for ebook formatting is around $100 – and I charge even more on my main site; the reason is because, if you're coding everything manually, and the author wants very specific styles or changes, it can take a lot of time.

So if you want more control and you want a designer to spend a lot of time on your ebooks, and you want someone to help you out or fix things when if you run into any problems, expect to pay more; but keep in mind you can do it for free or almost nothing if you keep things simple. (Some mainstream books don't even have indents on the first paragraph, although it's easy to do if you've prepared your word file the right way).

HOW TO MAKE A SMASHWORDS FILE

While Kindle takes up a big share of the ebook market, it's a good idea to have your book up in other stores as well, especially Apple iBooks. The easiest way to get in is to use a service like BookBaby or Smashwords. I prefer Smashwords because it's free and Mark Coker is a cool guy; they'll take your Word document but it needs to be clean before going through the "meatgrinder" (their automatic conversion software… it's pretty similar to the function I have on my site that converts to Kindle and Epub formats).

Luckily if you've already gotten your Word document ready as we discussed earlier (remove tabs, headers and footers, use H1 tags) you should just need to add the necessary copyright to the front and "Smashwords Edition" and it should be ready to go. (You can also just use the epub file you've made; you'll have to use Sigil to add "Smashwords Edition" to the front.)

As this can be a source of frustration however, it's another thing I would use Fiverr.com for. There are several providers who will make a Smashwords file from your Word document for about $10.

SOME OTHER FORMATTING RESOURCES

If you need more help or are shopping around, make sure you check out The Book Designer (Joel Friedman) and his formatting templates; Lisa DeSpain of ebookconverting.com; Suzanne Parrot's Unrulyguides.com; and 52novels.com.

PART THREE

Publish

Publishing a book is like
STUFFING A NOTE INTO A BOTTLE AND
HURLING IT INTO THE SEA

SOME BOTTLES DROWN, SOME COME SAFE TO LAND
WHERE THE NOTES ARE READ AND THEN POSSIBLY CHERISHED
OR ELSE MISINTERPRETED

OR ELSE UNDERSTOOD ALL TOO WELL
BY THOSE WHO HATE THE MESSAGE. YOU NEVER KNOW
who your **READERS** *might be.*

MARGARET ATWOOD

PUBLISH

Publishing for free isn't that hard; mostly, your book's success will come from the files you've prepared (cover and interior), and the reviews. Once your 'packaging' is right you just upload the files and you're done, which is why I'd never recommend a small press.

"An author who gives a manager or publisher any rights in his work except those immediately and specifically required for its publication or performance is for business purposes an imbecile."—George Bernard Shaw

"Authors today need a publisher as much as they need a tapeworm in their guts."

—Rayne Hall

EBOOKS

Make an account at Amazon KDP (Kindle Direct Publishing) and upload your mobi file and your ebook cover. Set your details and let 'er rip. In about 24 hours your book will be up for sale – but only on Amazon. If you want to get into other bookstores, you'll need to work with a distributor like Smashwords or Bookbaby.

Technically, your ebook should have an ISBN, but if you're only publishing on Amazon, you don't really need one. However, if you're publishing on other sites it may be required. You can pick one up from <u>Bowker</u> directly or buy a package of 10.

But you can also get a free one from Smashwords or other ebook distributors. ISBN numbers are references to your book details – including your publisher and the book format (ebook, print, hardcover). So you may want your ISBN to be listed with your pseudo-publisher name, to look more professional. But that will only matter if a bookstore or library is checking out your book. The majority of sales with come directly from readers through Amazon or another major ebook store – in which case you can often set the publisher info yourself, even if you got a free ISBN (it will display what you set, even though people who look up the details on Bowker may see that it's a free ISBN).

At this point, I wouldn't let these details bother you. They won't make a significant impact on sales; and sales are all that matter. Once you have big sales numbers and lots of reviews, nobody is going to care about whether it's self-published or what kind of ISBN you used.

THINGS TO CONSIDER ABOUT YOUR EBOOKS

The great thing about ebooks is that you can update them cheaply and easily – for example in a year or two you may have more books or a special promotion, or a new website. You can change the back or front matter of the ebook with the new details.

Ebooks are also very effective marketing – you can essentially give them away for free without losing money. You need to establish yourself as a bestseller by removing all buyer resistance, and low pricing is an easy way to accomplish this. They cost nothing to produce, so you want to get them out as widely as possible.

Pricing is tricky however: I had Book Marketing is Dead out at 99cents for a few months. I'd sell over 100 copies a month but was only earning 30%. I moved it up to $2.99 and sold less – but earning 70% made a big difference. Before I was selling about 40 copies, and earning roughly $15, each week. Now I'm selling around 20 copies and earning $40 each week. Interestingly though, I was getting better reviews at 99cents; at $2.99 I guess people expect more and are more likely to complain.

PRINT BOOKS

Your main choices for print books are Lightning source, Createspace or Lulu.

I always recommend Createspace over Lightning Source – LS offers no tangible benefits for self-publishing, higher setup fees and much more complications in the process of preparing files. The argument that LS can get your book in bookstores is entirely false: bookstores won't stock your book just because it's easy and available. Bookstores buy the bestsellers and they return what doesn't sell. Don't think LS is worth the investment with bookstores in mind: your sales and your reviews are what matter, and for that you can't beat Kindle, Createspace and Smashwords as distributors. Someday if your book is a bestseller and bookstores are clamoring for it, you can reassess whether LS is worth the investment. Lulu, while also cheap to set up, will cost more than Createspace.

You can get a free ISBN with Createspace, or pay extra to change the publisher name that displays on Amazon, or pay even more to change the listing on Bowker. Amazon/Createspace takes a big cut of your sales, but they also have the largest online bookstore. Lightning Source will give you more control over the bulk discount you offer, but it will take a lot of sales to earn back the initial set up fees. There are lots of arguments online, with facts and details, which seem to prove LS is more valuable in the long run. But it depends entirely on how many books you actually sell, and there is strong evidence showing that Createspace books will lead to more sales, even though LS books may be more heavily discounted. Also – I've had bookstores, libraries and universities order my books in bulk from CS at discount, so it can be done.

Rather than get bogged down in the details and controversy, just start out on Createspace – do it for free and get started. If you start selling thousands of copies a month, then you can see if Lightning Source makes sense for your book.

KEYWORDS, SUBTITLES AND CATEGORIES

Just because your book is available doesn't mean people can find it or buy it – so make sure you maximize your visibility by taking advantage of keywords, subtitles and categories.

Even a novel can benefit from a descriptive subtitle. Instead of "Eragon" it can be "Eragon: a dragon adventure story." Later if the book starts selling really well, you can remove the subtitle, but in the beginning it will help. If you can't fit keywords into the title or subtitle, use them liberally in the book description.

There are a lot of tricks and hacks to choosing subtitles and keywords. For example: start typing some keywords in the Amazon search bar (or Google) and check out the auto-complete options – they will show you commonly used search terms. If those are related, see if you can fit them in. You can also do more extensive keyword research or hire someone on Fiverr.com to do it for you.

THE PURCHASE PROCESS

Think about how readers find and buy your book: first, they see a guest post, or review, or advertisement that catches their interest. If the book cover looks professional, they'll click for more info and get directed to your website (or Amazon) for more details. If your description is amazing, they'll check the reviews. If those are good, and the price is reasonable, they may buy.

The other way it could happen is this: they are already on Amazon or another book site, browsing through a category, and your book shows up as a thumbnail (a small picture of the cover). If the cover catches their eye, they'll read the title and short description. If that sounds interesting, they'll click to see the sales page and read all the details and the reviews.

In both cases, if your cover is unattractive or unprofessional, they won't bother to read the details. And if the description is boring or poorly written, they won't bother to read the reviews. The book cover only has to be good enough to get them to the next step. The description needs to be even stronger. Get your description edited. Make it "Salesy" – copywriting is a skill with a long history of psychological manipulation. It's hard to do yourself if you aren't steeped in the tradition, but you can study great sales descriptions from other books in your genre. Assimilate and adapt, then hire an editor.

There are a lot of books and resources about "Gaming Amazon" and you can learn some clever tricks, but none of them are going to compensate for an unprofessional book cover (if you aren't sure about yours, send me an email, I'll let you know if it's good enough or if improving it could boost sales). And, in the end, your success is going to depend mostly on the quality of the book, and how many readers are interested in the genre.

Createspace also has cheap printing prices for POD books, so you can order 20 for events and won't pay much more than you'd pay ordering 500 copies at once (which you really shouldn't do). The only exception for this would be if you want your book cover to have fancy elements or speciality printing, like embossed text or spot-varnish. But you'd have to order a lot of copies, send a box to Amazon, and it would all be much more work. Unless you're making a specialty book (in which case you could also check out Blurb.com for more graphic projects) POD is really the way to go.

I feel like this section should be longer and I should include more resources... except that's really all there is. Publishing is about preparing the files, setting up your accounts on a couple of sites, uploading and setting the descriptions, keywords and details. Most first-time authors who fret about publishing are probably actually thinking about the formatting and book design, or about the marketing and sales aspects. If you're working with a small press the process will be considerably longer and more frustrating as you have to wait for them to do everything... but if you make your own accounts, making changes or updating files is quick and easy.

PART FOUR

Promote

In the old days

BOOKS WERE WRITTEN BY

MEN OF LETTERS AND READ BY THE PUBLIC.
NOWADAYS BOOK ARE WRITTEN BY THE PUBLIC

and read by **NOBODY**

OSCAR WILDE

PROMOTE

I wrote Book Marketing is Dead at the end of 2013, but some readers commented that they couldn't afford some of my tactics. So while I stand behind the message in that book, I'll try not to repeat myself here, and instead offer only powerful free tools you should be using to get the word out about your book. (By the way, if you want a free copy of that book, you can get it by joining the mailing list on my blog, www.creativindie.com.)

But keep in mind it's not only the things you do to sell books or the tools you use; often it's about who you are, how you present yourself. I have a very, very "soft" style to promotion. I rarely tweet or blog about my books, or email my list about them, more than once. I don't do much specific advertising. I rarely write guest posts. Yet my books (including this one) get dozens of reviews within a week and stay in the top ten of their categories pretty much indefinitely. While I could definitely be promoting more, I'm focused on building my platform rather than selling any one book. As a book designer, I've learned that having a great looking product matters about as much as your marketing or platform. (Although it won't save a bad book. A well designed, but badly written book will lead to high expectations but low satisfaction).

Before you start marketing, keep this in mind: ALL THAT MATTERS is sales and influence. There are books I don't think are very good. There are people that talk a lot and have a nice looking website and great elevated speeches about passion and art and life, but they don't really have any good content. They aren't teaching me anything. I like to think I'm better than they are, more educated, more talented, more capable. But none of those things matter – they can even be disadvantages. My pride may keep me from doing things I should be doing, out of fear of seeming crass, self-serving or stupid. I still focus on projects I like and ignore some I know would be far more effective, because "that's not the way I want to do things" or "that's not the way I want to be seen."

I hope my plans and strategies will be proven right; after all you can only be who you are and attract the kind of people who like what you have to say. But in the end all that matters is how much influence or power you have (a result of your relationships, authority and platform) and your sales (how much money you're making). And those two things reinforce each other.

Amendment: Sales and influence are all that matter short term, and you can start out big, grow strong, build a huge network and make a lot of money… but you'll do better long term if you can back it up with truly amazing content. At least I like to believe that. But, actually, amazing content is rare and it probably doesn't have as direct an impact on success as I like to believe. Plus, it's hard. You could focus on amazing content for years without increasing your sales or influence… and those may actually be more important. It's hard to tell. Somebody should do a study. My point is that a good book can be successful without much marketing, and a bad book can be successful with a big platform and a lot of marketing, but you need to shoot for the middle ground.

Think of book marketing like a bucket of water. You need to put readers in the bucket and keep adding water until they float to the top of the bucket and buy your book. Most internet marketers call this a "sales funnel." Something you'll quickly notice however, is not all the people you put in your bucket will stay with you long enough to make the sale. Some will ignore your bucket completely.

Some will jump in and dig around, but they'll disappear before buying the book.

Most authors think the way to sell more books is to keep adding people to the bucket through marketing, advertising and promotion – but this is mostly a waste of time and money. Why? Because there are holes in your bucket. Before you spend any serious investment on book promotion, you have to test your bucket with a little bit of water, to see where the leaks are, and patch them up as well as you can.

CHOOSE YOUR SALES FUNNEL

Once you get people's attention, where will you send them? Your website or blog? Your Facebook page? The book's Amazon page? There are reasons for choosing each. Amazon will look the most professional and reputable, so it will probably convert more people. However – most readers hearing about your book for the first time aren't ready to buy, so if you send them to the Amazon page, they may back out. All they wanted was some more information. Facebook pages have an advantage if you're using Facebook ads (it's cheaper to send someone to a Facebook page than an outside page; plus you can get traffic with smartly boosted posts). But even so, it's unlikely you'll make the sale from the first contact. In sales-speak, this is a "cold-call." It's the same as calling a stranger on the phone or knocking on someone's door and pitching your book. Very hard to do.

Since you want to build a relationship with your readers, it's probably best to use a blog or website – however, this only works if you have valuable content to offer. Think about it, what do you have for them besides the book you want them to buy? If you don't have anything, why should they come to your blog or website? What will they read? They aren't going to care about your book or author bio if they've never heard about you (unless, you have a brilliant, rock-star author bio and an amazingly powerful book description, plus a beautiful cover). You should have those things, and they will help, but you're still trying to sell a stranger a product they only heard about 5 minutes ago.

There are two ways to go about your website. The way I do it, is I offer a bunch of free content and articles about book publishing, making money from art and writing, and other business stuff. That gets traffic, which may turn into book sales or new subscribers (I'm actually not doing it very well, because I haven't put up a "Manifesto" or free offer that's compelling enough). Recently, however, I had a discussion with Matt Stone of Archangel Ink who told me that, since he's replaced his traditional blog with a one-page email opt-in form, even though he's lost 80% of traffic, he's getting much more email signups. Someone else I saw who launched quickly and has done this well, is Leanne Regalla of Make Creativity Pay. She started with no blog posts and only a short manifesto/free ebook download, then drove traffic with a bunch of guest posts. Rather than spending years writing content (like me) she built a healthy, targeted list around her theme in weeks.

You'll probably want to have some combination of these approaches, but make sure you focus on

- having something a value that people will want to sign up for
- organizing your site around a common theme or mission
- using guest posts to leverage other people's followings

WHO CARES ABOUT EMAIL SIGNUPS?

You should. There are two reasons why.

First, like I mentioned before, it's really hard to sell something to a stranger. It's far easier if you get them on your list and you slowly let them get to know you. You can use Mailchimp or Aweber to send pre-written content on a set schedule. For example, after they sign up, you send them a thankyou and a welcome email, maybe with their free gift. A week later, you send them a list of the most useful and important articles on your website. A week later, you send information about a meeting or event you're planning. Remember, you're not asking for anything, you're giving. You're trying to improve their lives. Ask how you can be helpful. I know this is tough for a fiction writer, but you have to figure out how to add value (a free short story every month? Tips on writing fiction? A writing class or peer-editing group?) Once people have gotten to know you, they'll be far more likely to buy your book later on.

Second, without a list, you'll never build any momentum for your author career. If you've just got one book and never plan to write another, that's fine – and the time and money you spend on marketing may sell some books, but as soon as you stop promoting, the sales will dry up. And if you do have another book or project, you'll have to start all over from scratch.

YOUR AUTHOR WEBSITE

Most authors make the mistake of treating their website like an online extension of themselves. They want the feeling and mood to match their personalities. And it can, a little, but spending a lot of money to hire a designer to make what you want is always a bad idea. The point of your website is to have a place to send people, and get them to take action. It's the first step in your sales funnel.

If it looks crazy, unprofessional or unorganized, or if people don't know what they should do, your website is a waste of space. Actually it's even worse than that – you'd be better off sending them straight to Amazon. While building your list is important, it's far too easy to get your website wrong.

"Design is not really a way for me to express myself. Design is a product that we produce for a client."

—Peleg Top

Don't hire someone and try to customize everything. Use Wordpress, find a theme that is pretty close to what you want, and just change the fonts, colors and header graphic or logo. Add a few plugins (I put a list of good ones here).

You can find a bunch of Wordpress templates on www.themeforest.com. Others I like are Themefuse.com, ElegantThemes, WooThemes, and ThemeTrust. Keep in mind the more fancy and stylish it is, the more likely someone else will use it. Don't keep it exactly the same. Also, a lot of Wordpress themes have a magazine style homepage, often with a moving slider. Most probably, you'll want to set your homepage to the normal blog page showing your most recent posts. So if you're checking out themes, make sure to look at the sample blog page to get the more minimal view of what it could look like. Disregard fonts for now, because you can use a Wordpress font replacement plugin like Google Fonts or Fontific to easily change the header styles (but don't go overboard). Simple is best. If you have good book cover art, see if your designer will make you a header. If not, use a nice Google font for the header and keep the graphics simple.

By the way – although most premium themes cost around $50, you can start with the default Wordpress Twenty-Thirteen or Twenty-Fourteen, get a header from Fiverr.com, and it will still look better than most author websites.

"The key utility measure is user happiness. Speed of response and the size of the index are factors in user happiness. It seems reasonable to assume that relevance of results is the most important factor: blindingly fast, useless answers do not make a user happy. However, user perceptions do not always coincide with system designers' notions of quality. For example, user happiness commonly depends very strongly on user interface design issues, including the layout, clarity, and responsiveness of the user interface, which are independent of the quality of the results returned." —Christopher D. Manning, Introduction to Information Retrieval

An anecdote: about a month ago I went through a phase of manic productivity and decided to launch two new businesses. For one, I found a theme, bought it, customized it, and it was ready to go in a few days. For the other, I found a beautiful theme that only had the Photoshop files: I bought it but then needed to hire a designer to code it to Wordpress. That cost $300 and took several weeks, but the guy I hired did a crap job of it, so I needed to hire someone else to redo it. It's still not done and it's been a major frustration. Try to find a theme that works: spend money on the header or logo, but don't try and build something from scratch.

Don't want to pay for your own web hosting? A year's worth of website hosting and a domain name will cost you about $20, and if you use a free theme, getting up and running with Wordpress can be very affordable.

But I apologize if I strayed from the core message of this book. While having your own online real estate is valuable, you can get a free website from Wordpress.org, blogger or other sites. In that case however, I'd probably just use a Facebook page – you can set your Facebook page up to collect emails as well, with a plugin. Or skip it altogether and focus on your Amazon page.

Let's go back to the Bucket of Water Metaphor. Before you do a huge guest post and flood your bucket with water, you want a little trickle of traffic, to see if your holes are plugged. If you're using Wordpress, you can use the free "Jetpack" site stats to keep track of your daily visitors. Right now I get about 200 a day. If I was selling 2 books a day, I might assume I'm converting 1 out of 100 (which wouldn't really be true, I'm probably getting those sales straight from Amazon). But, if I'm getting 2 new signups on my list every day, then the 1 out of a hundred is a solid ratio to start from. It isn't very good though. Which means, my website isn't really doing very much for me (something for me to improve on this year).

> "Great design = getting people to do what you want."
> —Seth Godin

However, there are other things to consider: a lot of my blog posts get shared widely by other websites. Repeated exposure to my name and my brand makes me more of an authority on the topics I write about. It also helps me build relationships on Twitter or Facebook, with other writers and bloggers who have their own networks. So while I'm not building my list very quickly or selling a bunch of books, my website still has some value. That said, www.creativindie.com has been up for a couple years and I have less than 3,000 subscribers. Meanwhile, www.DIYbookcovers.com has only been up a few months and already has almost twice that – because I giveaway a free package to help authors get started designing their own book covers. It's not a blog, it's just a one page site, focusing on a very specific niche topic and offering a solution. And although that list is growing quickly, and the people who signed up may enjoy some more tools and publishing resources, they are unlikely to buy my fiction books for example.

"Some websites are completely optimized for simple conversion, and it's easy to tell. The design centers on one clear call to action, a vivid lozenge labeled with a verb."

—Erika Hall, Just Enough Research

I'm actually not too worried about selling books, because I'm working on new, bigger books all the time that I expect will have wider readership. Also, I believe that after an initial push, most marketing is useless – a book will be successful or not based mostly on its own merits. But this is only after you've pushed the boulder. If you're starting from a square chunk of marble, it's not going to roll downhill. I'm mixing metaphors... Let me try and put them all together.

If you get your book in front of people, and they click over to your website, but then bail out – it's a hole in your bucket. If you get them onto your website and then actually get them to click over to the Amazon page (hooray!) but then they leave (oh no!) it's another hole in your bucket. The way to plug those holes is to send a specific amount of traffic to your website, or your Amazon page, and try to keep track of what's happening. Why are you losing them? What's going wrong?

If you're losing everybody on your website, try directing them to Amazon instead. How many buy the book? 5%? You need to have some sense of how big the "hole" is, so that you know whether or not new changes are an improvement.

> "Designers love subtle cues, because subtlety is one of the traits of sophisticated design. But Web users are generally in such a hurry that they routinely miss subtle cues."
> —Steve Krug, Don't Make Me Think: A Common Sense Approach to Web Usability

Your biggest holes are almost certainly your book cover, your book description, and your reviews, in that order. Your cover needs to be good, but really it only needs to be "good enough" to do its job. It has to grab attention by being beautiful and creating an emotional hook, and it has to look professional enough to be trustworthy. Readers won't spend a long time evaluating the cover, and it doesn't really factor into the purchase decision. It just moves them on to the next step – it gets them to read the sales description. If that is good enough, they'll read the reviews, and based on those three things, they'll decide whether or not to buy.

So by improving your cover, sales description and reviews, you can improve your conversion rate and plug the holes in your bucket, by degrees. Fix them a little, your conversion goes up to 20%. Make them all amazing, your conversion goes up to 50% (that's 10X more sales than you were getting at 5%). It's very hard to do all this on your own; you most likely don't have the design skills or the copywriting skills to improve your cover or the sales description. But don't try and start from scratch. Look at the bestsellers in your genre. Study their sales description. Isolate the sentence patterns and paragraph structure they are using. Cut out all the specific nouns and replace with your own book's details. It can't be identical, but take note of what they are doing right to improve your own. You can also hire someone on Fiverr.com to take a look at your website or amazon page for you and give you some pointers (or email me and I'll take a look).

HOW TO GET REVIEWS

"A writer hopes never to offend, but if he must, pray let him offend the gods before the reviewers."
—Chila Woychik, On Being a Rat and Other Observations

A lot of authors email me to check their Amazon page and I say, "Your cover and description look fine, but you don't have any reviews!" That's an example of a square chunk of marble. There's no point trying to promote it. It's going to be very hard to convince anybody else to share it, either. Your book has several "pain points" that are encouraging "buyer resistance." The bigger the price, the more resistance. The fewer reviews, the more resistance. The worse your cover or description, the more resistance. Do what you can with the cover and description, and then get some reviews up there asap. The easiest way to do this is to give the book away for free. Post it on your Facebook page or Website (yes, the whole thing). Email it to your friends and family. Tell them you don't want any Christmas or birthday presents, only book reviews.

Hopefully you'll get a handful. However, I should point out that asking friends and family for reviews is dangerous territory. They will feel pressured to write a good review because they care about you, so you're kind of asking them to lie, which is uncomfortable. Even if they love it, they'll be more concerned with your relationship than their real feelings about the book. So while you need to get some reviews up fast, and the only way may be to ask the people you already know, tread lightly. Make sure you don't ask for "Good" or "5-star reviews." That's dodgy. Tell them you'll be very happy with any review, even negative, you just want honest feedback (and you've got to be able to take it). Never respond or argue over a review.

The number of reviews matters almost more than the actual rating. A book with 10 five star reviews won't sell as much as a book with 100 reviews averaging 3.5 stars. Negative and positive reviews should be expected for any book that people are actually reading. In fact, negative reviews give credibility to all the positive reviews (which is why I set up the somewhat facetious website 1starbookreviews.com).

But you can also just give your book away for free for a while – either through Amazon's KDP select, or by setting the price to zero on Smashwords or another distribution site. Just make sure you put in the front and back matter, "I'm making this book for free for a limited time to get some reviews, so I'd appreciate it so much if you'd leave feedback – just your honest thoughts or responses would be so great." If you're doing a short free promo (like KDP select) focus on getting around 10 reviews before you give it away. Otherwise your downloads will start of too slow.

You can also buy reviews on Fiverr.com or other websites – I know that's a scandalous recommendation, and it's not a long term strategy, but as a way to plug the hole just long enough for real readers to take a chance on your book and leave genuine reviews, it undoubtedly works. For my first major book, I emailed hundreds of bloggers. I gave away Kindles. I sent out press releases and did radio shows. I got a lot of reputable reviews in the end, but it was a lot of work – especially in the beginning, when you're trying to get beta readers. If you're sending potential high-level reviewers to an Amazon page with zero reviews, you're jeopardizing your chances of getting them on board.

The angry rebuttal goes something like this: "It's totally wrong and immoral and unacceptable to pay for book reviews, EVER." But wait, then why do we have Kirkus, ForeWord and other sites that do extremely expensive paid reviews? Because they're honest and trustworthy? I'm not saying you should pay for lies. I'm not saying you should write the reviews yourself. But you can pay for people to read and leave honest, critical feedback of your book to get some reviews up quickly, and it doesn't have to cost hundreds of dollars. (I don't pay for reviews, because I've built up a big following and can get a bunch of reviews posted pretty quickly. But for writers just starting out, with no relationships or platform, I think at least considering the option is worth discussing.)

The practical issue: morality aside, having more reviews up, as long as they don't seem fake or cheesy, will help sales. However if readers are being misled, you will pay for it in the form of a backlash of negative reviews. Paid reviews that mislead are a bad idea.

The moral issue: if the reviews you paid for are honest and fair, and readers generally agree with them, and are happy the reviews convinced them to get the book (which they enjoyed), what does it matter where they came from? Who's being hurt?

Anyway, if you can't stomach it, don't do it. And it's probably best to exhaust other options first, and only use them as a last resort. But find a way to plug the hole before you try and market your book or promote a sales page with no reviews on it. Start small, get a few casual reviews, from anybody. Pitch the book to small bloggers. Offer incentives or rewards. Once you have some reviews, aim a little higher. Try to establish a network of people (maybe you're friends of a guy who's friends of a guy who's friends with a celebrity. Work your way up the chain).

Something I've started doing more recently, is giving away awesome stuff for free. For Book Marketing is Dead, I gave away 2 resort writer's vacations to the reviews voted most helpful during a set period. For this book, I'll email my list on DIYbookcovers.com and offer them full membership ($87 value) if they buy the book and leave a review. I'm also going to print out some inspirational posters and offer to mail them to people who review the book on Amazon (you can see what that offer looks like at the end of this book). The trick is, these kinds of "bribes" will only work if they are very related to the topic of the book. For a fiction book, maybe the heroine has a special magic necklace or hairpin or something. Maybe you can buy 100 of them on Alibaba.com direct from China. Maybe you can offer to read someone's star chart, or draw them a picture, or write them a poem. Maybe you can help other authors to critique or edit their work. Think of something you can buy cheaply or make or do that would interest readers of your book, and make them an offer.

It's likely to lead to more reviews than you would get otherwise, and it can be a fun way to engage readers. If it costs under $5 to buy or make and send (maybe with a handwritten thank you card) $50 will buy you 10 reviews. If you can only afford a few, say you'll only do it for the first 5 reviews posted before a certain date. (PS

– I don't think this will really work with a bookmark of your book, it needs to be something more general and less promotional. More about them, less about you).

A final thing to think about, is to make your book more interactive by partnering with other writers. For example, you could contact ten indie authors you notice on Amazon with books in a similar genre, and say something like "I'm trying to think of ways to market my book and noticed you have something in a similar genre; would you be interested in adding a short summary of your book and a link in the back of my book?"

You're basically giving them an opportunity to promote their book to new readers for free. As long as your book looks professional, some may take you up on it (they may offer to do the same for you, but that doesn't really matter). What matters is, now that your book refers people to their book, they are very likely to help plug your book to their fans, or review it.

For a book I'm working on (The Creative Brain on Drugs) I've contacted a bunch of companies who make "brain power" supplements. I let them know I'm writing about the history of artistic drug use and other creativity stimulants, and that I plan to review their product and link to their websites. I'm also setting up interviews with them. Once the book is out, all of those websites are very likely to promote the book or review it, because they're involved in the project, and sales of the book mean free publicity for them. Find a way to let other people be invested in your success.

(You may have noticed I'm using a ton of quotes in this book: after I publish I'll share these quotes one-by-one on Twitter and social media, and tag people with their handles if they have one. That gives me a whole bunch of social-media friendly, promotional content I can share, and will also get a lot of people involved).

SOME QUICK TIPS:
- Readers only see the cover. The cover only needs to be "pass/fail." It has to be good enough to grab their attention long enough for you to tell them more.
- Readers trust reviewers, not sales copy. Get 5 or 10 reviews up asap, by any means necessary.
- You need to think about your "Sales Funnel" and author career – you need to know what you want them to do, what your game plan is, where you want to be in one year.

HOW'S THIS FOR A BUSINESS PLAN:
1. You self-publish your book.
2. You do some FREE awesome content marketing and build your platform.
3. Your book sells 10,000 copies and gets 100+ positive reviews. You reinvest all your earnings in marketing or promotion and sell 50,000 copies.
4. A publisher reaches out and wants to sign you up with an advance of $50,000 (which you'll only turn down if you're on track to earn more than that on your own).

This is a pretty easy path to follow, if you have a good book and connect with the right readers. And it starts with no cash down – so in this section I'll focus on what you can do to sell your book and grow your platform quickly without shelling out any clams.

BEFORE YOU START…

Before you do any marketing or start telling people about your book, make sure your cover is as good as it can be. It really does matter more than anything else. That doesn't mean you have to buy an expensive one, but do get critical feedback. You can email me if you want and I'll let you know what I think.

Make sure your Amazon and other sales pages are finished and perfect. If you have a website, make it awesome.

FILLING THE BUCKET

So let's say you have spent some time and made your book, sales copy and website amazing. Your book is selling and earning natural reviews. Now you know that bringing in more traffic will lead to more sales.

WHAT MARKETING REALLY MEANS

Marketing means putting your product in front of people who may be interested, with enough incentive to get them to pay attention.

Here are the main ways it can happen:

YOUR OWN BLOG OR WEBSITE.

People browse for stuff and find your article. You can "fish" for readers by writing articles about stuff they are interested in. Lists are easy, for example "top 10 best romance heroines ever" or "7 steamy office erotica books of 2013." You don't need to include your own book, although you may want to mention it at the bottom or recommend it to them.

Your blog or website should have one main "call to action" – probably trying to get them to sign up on your list. Don't try to get them to do so many things, or give them too many options. Getting them to sign up to your Facebook page is mostly useless and not worth the effort (plus, if you have a low number of likes, you're actually using negative social proof to undermine your credibility). For more on Facebook, check out this article I wrote recently. http://www.creativindie.com/why-having-a-facebook-author-page-for-your-book-is-mostly-useless/

GUEST POSTING ON OTHER BLOGS OR WEBSITES.

It takes a lot of time for your blog to pick up steam though, so people probably won't find your articles unless they're super specific. An easier way is to guest post on other websites with a bigger audience.

All you need to do is make a list of blogs or websites in the same genre or field, or devoted to a relevant topic, and contact them about writing a guest post. It's best if you've done research and already have the article prepared. It's best if your website is set up and looks professional. You want to keep the email very short and sweet.

If you want to increase your chances of success, follow the blog owner on Twitter or Facebook, like and share some of their content and comments for awhile; then when you contact them they'll have an idea who you are.

ADVERTISEMENTS ON SITES WHERE THEY SPEND THEIR TIME.

Advertising can be powerful, but it's hard to actually make more than you spend. You can use Google ads to target specific websites, or use it to show up whenever people are searching for relevant terms. I mostly use advertising if I'm promoting something fun or free, like a contest or giveaway, as it's more likely to get traction. You can also check out ProjectWonderful.com for very cheap advertising.

A lot of advertising is plain ignored... or you need to keep it up long term to make an impact. If your book is already selling well but you want a boost, and you want to target very specific types of people, advertising can be good for this (especially Facebook ads, where you can target people who liked a similar book or genre).

Also, since you shouldn't be talking about your book all the time on social media, if you can't be bothered to provide useful content, advertising is one way to go, if you have the budget.

For more advertising tips check out this article:

http://www.creativindie.com/everything-you-wanted-to-know-about-advertising-your-book-book-promotion-through-google-facebook-and-more/

MAKING FRIENDS ONLINE

The best strategy for promoting books is to have a lot of friends with big networks. The way to do it is to add them on Facebook or Twitter, and reply or comment when they share stuff. Keep it casual. Don't try too hard. Don't be a kiss-ass. Just treat them like normal human beings. Find a way to provide value to them.

A COMMUNITY, NOT A SOAPBOX

Building an author platform is hard work, and unlikely to be successful unless you're a rock star. If you bleed charisma and are unusually attractive, charming and witty, being the center of attention may come naturally to you. But if you're like me (a little uncomfortable in the spotlight) shouting for attention will seem unnatural. But that's OK – don't focus on you. Focus on creating a space that affirms other people. Focus on building a community other people join because it says something about themselves. Make a movement, a mission, a revolution. Make a call to action.

It's hard to be the leader and have people follow. It's much easier to just share your likes and interests with other like-minded people.

Instead of sharing your supernatural thriller, ask questions like "if you could have any supernatural power, what would it be?" Review movies or TV shows about supernatural characters. Make an online personality test of some kind. The trick is to create the kind of content that the right type of readers will enjoy. Try to engage them, not sell to them.

CONTESTS

Contests can be fun, but make it interesting. It needs to be easy enough for people to do, with a tangible prize that people want; but also connected with your book enough that you don't get a bunch of random people.

Book giveaways often aren't enough. (Unless say, you partnered with ten other indie authors and made a big prize of 10 novels). Always be thinking bigger. Contact local stores or organizations and see if they're willing to donate something as a prize (a lot of them will be).

BOOK COVER REVEALS

Nobody will care about your book cover until they've read your books. So if you don't have a large following, who have already read your books, a book cover reveal won't do much for you. (It won't sell the book, since the book probably isn't out yet. And nothing is happening, because there's no action).

If you're ready to show off your book cover, great – but think of a way to do it that is more interactive. For example, I always recommend authors ask on Facebook or Twitter for feedback on cover art. Give them 3 or 4 samples to choose from. Even if you've already decided, letting other people comment on which ones they like builds interaction and is much more powerful than simply showing your final cover. Let them be involved in your publishing process.

BLOG TOURS

I'm not sure how I feel about blog tours, but in general I think the people who visit indie book review sites are probably indie authors (not book buyers). Getting featured on ten blogs doesn't mean much if it doesn't lead to real readers or book sales. The same goes for most book marketing services that claim to have 50,000 followers or page views: the people who follow or visit are probably other authors trying to sell books, not potential readers. Advertising your free book giveaway on a big site like BookBub or KindleDailyNation will do more than getting on various blogs.

Also, you want to be featured on specific blogs that are more targeted to your readers, rather than general sites. If you are writing romance, and there's a specific blog tour that hits the main romance review sites, then it may be worthwhile. One thing to consider, is if the blogs in question have a high page rank and they'll all link back to your site, you'll be getting some "link juice" which may help your own websites ranking.

PRESS RELEASES

I don't think it's worthwhile for authors or book promotion. But you might want to do it anyway, especially if you:

A) have a non-fiction book or
B) are promoting some kind of business

Trying to write a press release to get more sales by drawing attention to your book (a promotional PR) is not likely to work, because people won't share something that has no inherent value (and is basically advertising).

So if you write about your new book as a product and say:

1. This is what it is
2. This is what it does
3. This why/where you should buy it and how much it costs...

Few people will want to repost that on their site because it's not real news: news is what happens.

News has to be interesting. It has to matter to people – not only to people looking to buy a particular thing. It CAN be news if it solves a problem, as in "Learn this amazing new way to shed pounds on a diet of chocolate milkshakes."

In Author 101, Rick Frishman says "To attract press, you need headlines about Money, Sex, Health, Controversy. You need bold, daring, risqué headers. Take chances; be provocative, naughty and controversial."

It can solve a problem. It can be about something new and interesting (really amazing) that will be appreciated by people. It can be that you won an award (although this probably won't work so well, unless it's the Pulitzer...)

It can be about a project, event or community (the bigger the better) especially if you're doing something that helps others.

It won't be shared just because somebody wants to do you a favor; it will be shared based on the amount of traffic it may get or how much readers will appreciate it. If you're trying to get people involved or to participate in something, make it fun and easy: Seth Godin writes in his post 8 Email Failures, "The thing you need me to do better be fun, worth doing and generous. If it's not, I'm not going to do it, no matter how much you need me to do it."

So the topic matters.

But people won't click it without a killer headline.

The headline has to present the story, the benefits, the news, in a way that tickles the imagination and hooks attention.

It can be surprising or bizarre: "Man saves drowning dolphin."

It can be a list (sometimes overcoming objections): "7 ways to get healthy (without dieting or exercise!)" It can be a question: "Do you make these common writing errors?"

Although writing a press release may not directly help you sell more books, it's worth thinking about (and practicing) how to spin your news so that its newsworthy and shareable, and crafting headlines that get clicked.

POSTCARDS, BUSINESS CARDS, ETC.

Business cards are handy and convenient when you're telling someone about your book. You can't fit much information, so you need to think carefully about what to include. Hopefully your book cover is already awesome; in which case you can just use the cover art on one side and a few details on the back.

If you plan to give one out to everybody (including a ton of strangers) you may not want your email or phone number on there. Often you'll want to focus on sales; so instead you'll have your winning tagline or catch phrase, and your most powerful review. You can say something simple like "now available on Amazon" or "available at all major bookstores" (even if they don't stock the book, readers can go into any bookstore and request that they order it).

If you have an offer on your website and are trying to drive email list signups, you may want to mention it. Passing out cards is a lot of work though, and you'll have to get new ones for each book, so you may consider getting a more general "author" card for you, with your email, phone and website, and then printing other promotion materials for each specific book.

Bookmarks are fun but they're too small; they make for OK little gifts... but you want them to look nice and not be "salesy"; they should mostly be decoration, maybe with the book title and a tagline or catchphrase. The size is pretty good however for banners or headers (2"x6" @ 300dpi makes a web banner that's 1800px – most standard website headers or banners are only around 1200px these days). In turn, they make great images to add to a Facebook or Twitter post... just change the text a little or use a different quote, and you have new promotional material to share.

For events, you can use a business card stand to share your cards, but I recommend getting postcards made. With a 5"x7" postcard, you can basically use your full front and back cover (which should already be carefully edited with your best sales copy, reviews and website info) and print high quality postcards. A stack of these make it easier for browsers to grab more complete info about your book (and introverts may actively avoid you if you're handing out business cards, while if you give them some space and they're interested, they'll help themselves to a postcard).

The other great thing about postcards is that you can just leave stacks lying around wherever readers congregate – like coffeeshops or bookstores. For bigger events, you could use 4" x 9" rack cards (kind of like a one-side flyer) or get a bigger poster printed of the cover art.

Choose what materials will fit best with your personality and marketing style.

WHERE TO GET THE BEST PRINTING

I use Overnightprints.com for almost everything; their prices are low, uploading files is pretty easy and the quality is great. They have a large range of products. If you need a specific size you can go to their website and download a Template for the size you need.

For most things, the 15pt card stock is very firm and nice. For very expensive, premium luxury products (maybe a real-estate or investment book) getting materials printed 110# premium card stock will have a heavier, better quality feel.

Another thing I love about Overnightprints.com is that they make it easy to use "Spot-varnish." Just like book covers, you can choose Gloss (full UV) or No Gloss (matte). Usually, for colors and graphics, gloss is best. For clean, solid white stuff or non-fiction, matte can be more professional.

Spot-varnish, however, makes most of the card matte but with a bit of varnish just over the text, which makes the text a little shiny. The effect is cool and very professional. All you have to do to get it, is save your file as a PDF, then remove all the images and change all the text to solid black with no effect. Make sure the text is in exactly the same place. Save that file as another PDF, and upload it to Overnightprints.com for the spot varnish file.

I added some templates for these things (including some "sell-sheets") on the free and member area of http://www. diybookcovers.com, so you can grab those and make your own files to upload to Overnightprints.

10 MOST POWERFUL THINGS YOU CAN DO FOR FREE

These are the things I would focus on that have the most powerful impact on book sales.

1. Revise your book cover or description.
2. Get reviews. Keep begging and emailing until you have ten.
3. Give the book away for free; make sure you announce it on all the free book websites, Facebook pages and Reddit subboards.
4. Make a list of 25 popular blogs in your genre, that your readers like to visit. Pitch them a guest post. Keep working on these until you have 25 guest posts out there.
5. Write 25 articles on your own blog or website. Share them on Facebook and Twitter.
6. Find a bunch of beautiful images (you can search for desktop backgrounds, or find stuff on Deviantart). Whenever you post something to Twitter or Facebook, use an image – they're much more likely to get liked and shared. A variation of this, is to add a quote over the picture. You can pull amazing passages from your book and add them over the image. People are much more likely to share the picture+quote than to share something flagrantly promotional. (I'm going to put up some MS Word templates to make this easier soon). Make 10 and post one every 3 days for a month.
7. Plan an interesting event around your theme, genre or about self-publishing. Make it big and newsworthy. The actual event matters less than the reportage of the event. So make it look like a big deal, even if nobody shows. (For example, you can take a picture of you standing at a fancy podium on a huge stage… even if the audience is empty).

8. Go to events and make friends with other indie authors in your area. If there aren't any events – make one: make a Facebook page called "Support group for indie authors in (your town)" or "The self-publishing association of (your town)" and have a monthly meeting.

9. Write another book. And another, and another. Write mini-books, and short stories. Get as much content up on Amazon as you can.

10. Review other people's books. Buy and read as many as you can. Review them on Amazon and on your own blog. Promote and help as many other authors as you can. Build up your social karma.

11. I'll throw in an extra one, that I was just reminded of by this very awesome article: <u>17 advanced methods</u>.

    Find 15 self-published books in your genre that are doing pretty well but not super amazing. Search for them in Google to find blogs that have written about them: contact the blogs and say "I noticed you shared this book, I have something similar, can I send you a copy? I think you'll enjoy it." Do the same thing on Twitter: search for the book, find people who have mentioned it or shared it, send a direct message asking if they'd like yours as well. Always offer an ebook or PDF first, but say you could also send a print book if they prefer. (Giving out ebooks like this is free and easy).

If you do all these things and your book still isn't selling at all, you've probably still got a square chunk of marble, which means either your book doesn't look good, or the story isn't good enough, or the target readership isn't large. In which case more marketing is not going to help. If you give it a big, firm push and it doesn't go anywhere all on its own, pushing harder, or longer, isn't going to overcome your problems.

> "Persistence can look a lot like stupid."
> —Kristen Lamb, Are You There Blog? It's Me, Writer

If you want quick feedback about your website, sales page or book cover, you can send me an email and I'll try to take a look at it (I probably won't have time to help fix it, but I can identify red flags).

You should also check out this page, it has a whole bunch of awesome articles on book marketing.

http://chrismcmullen.wordpress.com/index-of-marketing-posts/

Final tips: Most of the people talking about book marketing don't know what they're talking about. A lot of them are successful authors who sell a lot of books because they write great books. Others are not very good writers that have learned to market the hell out of their books because they have to. Others are famous authors whose books got successful decades ago and now give book marketing advice even though they can barely use the internet. If you're trying to market books online, you should really be studying things like growth hacking or content marketing. You should be learning from the bloggers who make a hundred grand on each book launch. Don't assume other authors who talk about book marketing know what they're doing. Also test, and keep in mind marketing only works if you have a well designed product and you're putting it in front of people who want it. Marketing is easy if you've spent more time focused on making a product people want.

LAST WORDS
FROM SMART PEOPLE

I like to keep in mind that I may be wrong about everything. So I asked some of the people I know with a lot of experience writing, formatting and publishing books for their thoughts on these questions:

1. #1 tip for writing the book (software, motivation, revising)?
2. #1 tip for formatting for print or ebook, and/or publishing?
3. #1 tip for free or cheap book marketing or promotion?
4. #1 piece of advice for self-publishing authors?

Some of their advice may even directly contradict my own. That's OK.

> "Do I contradict myself? Very well,
> then I contradict myself, I am large,
> I contain multitudes."
> —Walt Whitman

Here are their replies. Some of it may be repetitive, but it will give you a good understanding of what a whole bunch of smart people are doing, or like or recommending.

~ Debbie Young ~

Self-published author and Commissioning Editor of ALLi's
www.selfpublishingadvice.org

(1) As in the old saying, "the best way to get something done is to just do it" – no book will get written without hard graft, so clear blocks of writing time and set yourself a schedule. Don't beat yourself up when you fail to meet specific self-imposed deadlines – that'll kill your creativity. But there's no magic bullet that will substitute for perseverance.

(2) My pet hate: Don't leave spaces between paragraphs – it is infuriating for anyone reading the e-book, especially if your paragraphs are short, because it wastes screen space and requires more page-turning than strictly necessary.

(3) Create, maintain and regularly update (at least weekly) a focused author website – it's your shop window, open to the world – using the free Wordpress.com software. If you take the time needed to learn all its tricks via its excellent help sections and forums, you'll find Wordpress very flexible and powerful, and it's all absolutely free, if you use the entry-level version. If you have at least a tiny budget, add a custom URL (e.g. www.authordebbieyoung.com as opposed to www.authordebbieyoung.wordpress.com) to look more professional. Otherwise there's no software cost, no set-up fee, not even a hosting charge. Worried about learning new software? Don't be. If you're up to formatting a Word document, you can manage Wordpress.

(4) Make your book the best it can be before you publish it. Self-publishing is not an excuse for cutting corners.

~ Chris Casburn ~

www.creaturesofchichester.com

(1) Get a good beta reader to review each chapter as you go along. Don't wait until the end. Make sure he/she is not family, honest and able to tell you the truth!
(2) Cut out dedications, etc. if you've added these to a tree-book and add a request to review on Amazon at the end.
(3) If writing a kids book you must do school visits and in the UK they will pay you too!
(4) Form a group with other local authors to share costs of stands at book fairs etc. – and it's not so lonely!

~ Ellie Stevenson ~

The Haunted Historian: haunting the page across time.
elliestevenson.wordpress.com

(1) Write first and edit later. The main thing is to get the story down in full. Perfecting the language and rhythm comes later.
(2) Poor formatting can ruin a reader's experience of your story. A lot of traditional word processing software can introduce quirks which won't come out well on an e-reader. You need to address this.

(3) Build relationships with people on Facebook and Twitter. This will take time but will also introduce you to fellow authors. Share information that readers will find interesting, related to your book. Pinterest is also a great way to showcase your book visually.

(4) Join the Alliance of Independent Authors for great advice and a good network of fellow professionals.

~ Jeannie van Rompaey ~

http://www.jeannievanrompaey.co.uk

Once you feel you've taken your book as far as you can, hire a professional creative editor. You don't have to take on board everything she says. It's your book, but consider the comments carefully and don't be too proud to change some things.

~ Laurence O'Bryan ~

Author of the guide to social media – Social Media is Dynamite

Take a look at socialmedia4writers.com for a weekly magazine and archive of online book marketing ideas, for free.

~ Orna Ross ~

READ THE CONTRACTS. Know what you're selling, how much it costs and how you'll be paid. Know what you're buying, how much it costs, how you will pay. (Percentage or lump-sum). If percentage, percentage of what, net or gross? discounts? And term. Always look at the term.

~ Jim Kukral ~

Founder, Author Marketing Club

(1) Use Google docs. It's free, and you can write from any location (coffee shop, home, poolside) with an Internet connection. It lets you keep one master document in the cloud at all times.

(2) Technically you could upload a Word doc directly to Amazon, but you should pay to have a properly formatted eBook so it just reads nicer. You want to look professional, yes?

(3) Take advantage of your free days in Amazon KDP Select. Include a proper call to action in your book at the end to get the reader to join your email list so you can sell them on future books.

(4) Get the book done and publish! It will never be perfect. The longer you wait; the longer you don't have the opportunity a good book brings to your reputation or career.

~ Children's author Karen Inglis ~

selfpublishingadventures.com; kareninglisauthor.com

A couple of print publishing tips from a children's author...

Print books – if using images use Insert > Picture to place them in the file. Don't just copy and paste them into the file. Also don't resize them inside the Word document. Insert the file size you need. (I use black and white images for children's books.) This rule may also apply for ebook images.

If you're creating a children's picture book for print, be aware that you cannot get silk paper finish from Createspace or Lightning Source. The paper finish is good but it's not the sticky-finger proof variety that you see on the shelf in bookshops.

~ Dan Holloway ~

Author of Self-publishing With Integrity

(1)　Never write for anyone but yourself.

(2)　For print books, on a basic level, pay attention to pagination –the font, the pointage, the positioning; more generally, always leave sufficient margins.

(4)　Never take yes for an answer. If too many people are happy with what you are doing, you're doing it wrong – it never pays to be too close to the centre of the bell curve

~ Walt Morton ~

Author of American Ghoul

(1)　Accept the idea that producing a book is a DAILY PROCESS. You don't need to have every part perfectly figured out in advance before you begin. That would require literary genius plus marketing and design genius. The process will go more smoothly if you work at it steadily, every day, keeping your mind in the game and allowing the book time and space to grow and evolve.

(2)   You will be happy if you write a clean simple story that does not rely on any tricky formatting, fonts, italics, etc. It's almost impossible to make something graphically complicated look good on every e-reader, phone, kindle and other device. KEEP FORMATTING SIMPLE.

(3)   STICK TO THE INTERNET. You may be tempted to take out a print ad in the New York Times. It will never pay for itself. All the best promotions are online, because online your potential readers are just one click away from a purchase, a download, and a review. Plan on trying various things (bookbub, KDP, giveaways, etc.) there is no one perfect way unless you are famous and already have 2 million facebook followers.

(4)   BE PROFESSIONAL. Spend 95% of your efforts producing the best fiction you can, and that includes more time writing, revising and editing it to make it easy to read and entertaining. Work with at least one editor and proofreader. Make a completely professional error-free presentation and then readers take you seriously and give you money. Only 5% of your time should go into marketing, because there are limits to what you can achieve. If you are a writer – just write. You are better off with 10 books than 1 book you have marketed like crazy.

~ James Ventrillo ~

Reader's Favorite

"Lady in the Water," have you seen it? It was that movie about a mermaid that lived in Paul Giamatti's pool. It was written, directed and even co-starred M. Night Shyamalan. Night based the movie on a fairytale he made up for his kids. He was hot off the success of his previous movies and presented the story to his distributor, Disney, who footed the bill for his previous hits. Disney took one look at the script and had Night escorted out of the building.

Night ignored Disney's criticisms and did what any multi-millionaire would do--he paid for it himself. The movie bombed and Night had to eat Ramen for the next six months. Why am I telling you this story? Because books, just like movies, are supposed to go through a rigorous production process. For movies, dozens of people have to read the script and approve it, making improvements along the way until it is ready to be filmed. Then even after the movie is made it is edited, where entire scenes, subplots and even characters are completely removed. Next it is screened, and audiences critique the film, often sending it back for more changes until it is finally ready for mass release.

But Night did not do that. He bypassed the system because he could, and he paid the price. As a self-published author you are also bypassing the system.

Note from Derek: I pulled this story from readersfavorite.com because I love the message. James continues by recommending you produce a quality product, get it edited, enter book award contests, "attend book fairs and conventions, build a website, get on Facebook and Twitter, and start getting the word out about your book. In time, word of mouth will hopefully take over for you and your book will go viral." Note the major emphasis on "hopefully" – if you didn't create a product that people like, by considering the readers and potential market, no such thing will happen.

~ Matt Stone ~

www.archangelink.com

(1) My top tip for writing a book is to immerse yourself in the thing. I call it "binge writing." I try to write an entire draft in as few days as I can from start to finish. You can spend as much time as you like revising, but the actual creation of the thing – and this is even more true for fiction than nonfiction, although I apply this to nonfiction – should happen fast. I always drag ass when I first get started on any big project, because I lack momentum. Momentum is everything. I think that's all writer's block is: a lack of momentum. But once you get momentum, take advantage of it. When I'm really cranking on a project, 5,000 words gets written in the same amount of time, and with the same amount of effort, as 500 words did on the second day. Live, eat, sleep, and breathe that book from the first sentence to the last. Otherwise you're likely to spend more time trying to figure out what you've written already when you sit down to write than you will actually writing.

(2) I think the most important thing when it comes to publishing is making sure you've got a solid launch plan, and that everything is tight. Like Derek points out in Book Marketing is Dead, you have to get the title, cover, book description, and other basic fundamentals rock solid. If not, don't bother trying

to sell it. Get it perfect, then enter the market with as big of a splash as you possibly can. The sales you get in that first week will determine a lot of the future success of that book. Don't botch the launch! Oh wait, Derek hates exclamation points and capitalized text, let's mess with him: "DON'T BOTCH THE LAUNCH!!!!!!!!"

(3)   For free book promotion, you've got to really hit up those book deal Facebook groups. Naht! Listen to this carefully, as this simple tip can and will completely change your life, not just for book-writing, but for all things relating to internet-based business if you choose to take it seriously... It's better to make a strong connection with one important person than it is to make weak connections with tens of thousands of unimportant persons. The internet is filled with thousands of successful bloggers, social media dynamos, experts, and entrepreneurs with great influence. I'm not talking about the people you've heard about before. Those people have agents and bodyguards and a huge wall of people trying to filter out lil' folks like you. But those mid-sized people are a gem. They get lots of emails, but not enough to be unable to answer yours. They will give you the time of day, answer your questions, and let your voice be heard. Make. A. Connection. If you want someone to do a favor for you, do a favor for them. Anything. Develop a connection and a rapport with them. Almost all of the big favors I have done for people myself were in response to a cold email. Almost all of the big favors done for me began with me sending out a cold email. I recently just built a highly profitable business in three months with two emails sent to the right two people. 20 minutes. $0.00. Believe it. This is not a scammy thing either unless you make it one (if you do you won't get anywhere with this strategy).

The two people I contacted are both going to make thousands of dollars this year based on the favors I did for them. Get involved with creating mutually beneficial relationships with the right people. Work nonstop for a month for free for them if you have to. They spent years to build the audience they have built, and in a month you can buy yourself a ticket to a powerful endorsement/referral to that giant audience they spent a half decade building. All the free book Facebook promo groups on earth will never do as much as one powerful endorsement from someone with 5,000 daily site visitors, 50,000 followers on Facebook, and a mailing list of 20,000. Never. And people with that kind of audience have an endless abyss of connections with others just like them. Anyway, if you want people to find out about you and become interested enough to read your work, find the people out there with a strong relationship with tens of thousands of readers, and attack them—not with SPAM or brown-nosing—but with radical sincerity, loyalty, and the offer of unthinkable favors asking nothing in return. Not everyone will reciprocate, but most will, it only takes one, and it doesn't cost anything. Plus, you get to know really cool people that way. You get to like and be liked by someone else. That's fulfilling. Empty SPAM marketing is empty and will crush your soul. Just having people of influence know your name is money in the bank as far as I'm concerned.

(4)   My biggest tip for authors is to always be true to what you want to do. Nobody was ever truly successful forcing themselves to do something they hate. Even if they made money, they sacrificed years of their lives. You think trading years of your life for money is success? If I could make you a millionaire tomorrow, but the downside was that you were

going to die in five years for accepting the money, would you take that offer? Geezus I hope not. When you are doing exactly what you want to be doing—when you are immersing yourself in exactly what you want to be immersing yourself in—you will go much farther much faster. You think I have to motivate myself to write, mentor authors, or to do the things I do? No way. I have to motivate myself to go to sleep, to eat, and to go outside. I really love what I do that much, and I refuse to spend time doing things that I don't want to do. That's why I'm so successful. Even if you didn't make a lot of money by spending every day doing what you want to do at the exclusion of that which you find unpleasant, your life would still be great. Odds are, you'll get freaking rich doing what you love—building exceptional skills, knowledge, talent, and expertise in whatever arena you are pouring all of your passion into. Spending tens of thousands of hours engrossed in something you love simply leads to the cultivation of something rare and exceptionally valuable.

~ Sean Platt ~

The Self-Publishing Podcast

(1) Use Scrivener. It's the best writing software I've used in six years of writing every day, with millions of words produced. It is outstanding, and will save you countless hours in composition, editing, formatting, and general execution.

(2) That's a very general/nebulous question, with four very different branches to the tree, so I'll stick with print. Many (MANY) writers think they need to be in print. You don't. Print

accounts for relatively few sales in the scheme of things. As long as you know why you want your book in print (promotion, fan love, ego, price anchoring, etc.) it can be a great idea, but doing it "just because" rarely is.

(3)   Have something (exceptional) free that makes it easy and frictionless for a new reader to find you and try you out.

(4)   Write. Publish. Repeat. Like we always say, keep writing. Don't stop. One book will never make a career.

~ Joanna Penn ~

www.thecreativepenn.com

(1)   Use Scrivener and the word count tracking so you can monitor progress every day. Seeing the little bar turn from red to green as I reach my word count goal is fantastic. I also write on a physical wall diary and get a star sticker if I go over 2000 words. It's a behaviour encouragement chart for children basically, but it works for the writer's brain too!

(2)   I use Scrivener to output .mobi and .epub and that has been fine for Kindle, Kobo and iBooks, but for Nook I hired a formatter as the upload process is so sensitive. I also hire a print interior designer in order to have a quality final product.

(3)   Marketing is sharing what you love with people who enjoy hearing about it. So just start sharing your passions and obsessions on the site of your choice and, over time, you will attract like minded people.

(4)   Be patient and think of this as a five year project. There's no need to sell a gazillion copies of your first book. In fact, you probably don't want to, because you will get better with

more writing. If you just take little steps every day, write 1000 words, write a blog post, connect with one person on social media, then in five years, your life will have changed. Mine certainly has!

~ Shelley Hitz ~

Founder of www.trainingauthors.com

(1)   I am a fan of outlining a book, whether fiction or nonfiction, to help finish a project. Lately, I have been using mind mapping to outline my book chapters as it makes it super easy to move things around, edit it, and then export it to Word or a text file so I can put the outline in my book template.

After I create the outline of my book, I sometimes use the free project management software, Asana.com, to plan out a tentative schedule and deadline of when I want to have each section done. This works best when I am working with another person on a project, like Heather Hart and I did on our book, "How to Get Honest Reviews" or when working with a coach or accountability partner. I have been using Asana with my monthly coaching clients as well to help them successfully meet their goals and to keep them accountable. You can see a brief video tutorial I created about Asana here: https://www.youtube.com/watch?v=N3ricbq3qSQ

(2)   I recommend authors create a formatting system that works best for them and then use that same system over and over as they publish new books. At this time, I have published over 30 books in eBook, print and audiobook formats. For books in a series or similar genre, I create a book template with similar

front matter and back matter. This allows me to then do a few simple edits for the next book in the series and start writing right away in my template which saves me a ton of time.

Make sure that you check your formatting after uploading to the various platforms. For example, if you publish a Kindle eBook on KDP, I recommend reviewing the .mobi file they give you on your Kindle device, Kindle app, and on the cloud online. One book I published looked fine on my Kindle device, but had formatting issues when viewing it on the Kindle app. Therefore, take the time to make sure your formatting is done correctly.

(3)   My best free book marketing recommendation is to consider using the KDP Select program. This is not a great strategy for every book and every author. However, we have had success using it for some of our books. You do need to invest your time promoting it and we recommend submitting your book to sites that promote free books. I share my 11 step checklist for organizing a KDP Select promotion as well as 76+ places to promote your book here: http://www.trainingauthors.com/kdpselect

(4)   In some ways, for an author, the finish line is publishing your book. However, that is when the book marketing just begins. No matter where you are in your journey of writing, publishing or marketing your book; I encourage you to persevere. In the words of Winston Churchill... "Never, never, never give up!"

~ Joel Friedlander ~

www.thebookdesigner.com; www.bookdesigntemplates.com

(1) Try out "distraction free" writing environments like iAWriter, Ommwriter or others. You'll be amazed at how much work you'll get done.

(2) Print books follow specific, industry-standard rules, and following those rules will help your book reach greater acceptance with book publishing professionals like book reviewers, buyers, and media types too.

(3) Recognize that, for nonfiction authors, an authoritative, engaging, and helpful blog in your subject area is about the best and most cost-effective online marketing tool ever invented.

(4) Decide up front whether you are publishing for your own enjoyment, to sell tons of books, or to help establish yourself in some other work you do. This decision will guide you throughout the process.

~ Mick Rooney ~

The Independent Publishing Magazine

(1) Scrivener is a great tool for the writing process, and taking your book to print and/or ebook publication. Once you have the basic framework of story and plot, push on and complete the first draft. Don't stop to rewrite what you already have written.

(2) Examine other professionally produced books. Keep formatting simple. Don't be extravagant with fonts and sizes. And above all, if you use MS Word as a raw file for conversion to ebook, use the built in formatting options for paragraph indents and don't use a double-space at the start of every new sentence.

(3) Free or heavily discounted promotional offers are great to give your book an early start, but don't fall asleep at the marketing wheel. Free works best in short strategic bursts. Offering free books for long periods of time after release is like leaving your Christmas tree up until Easter!

(4) Self-publishing means taking on all of the responsibility of managing your book project. It doesn't mean you have to – or should – take on the tasks of self-editing and self-designing your book! Always use professional services and advice if a task is outside of your skillset.

~ Mars Dorian ~

Visual Storyteller, www.marsdorian.com

(1) Finish what you start – only then will you improve your craft. So don't start the next book if the first isn't finished yet.

(2) Add sufficient white space between paragraphs or chapters. Nothing kills reading joy (and grows eyes tired) more than one endless chunk of text.

(3) CTA – Call To Action at the end of the book. The best marketing happens when your customers talk about your book, and a good way to make them talk about it is to tell

them at the end: "If you like my book, please recommend it to your family and friends."

(4) Try to write a story that only you can write. The world doesn't need another me-too copycat, the world needs original and fresh storytelling.

~ Brendan McNulty ~

www.NowNovel.com

We see motivation as being equally as challenging as having the inspiration to write, and so we have a process that we go through to inspire and support people through their writing. We've found that the most important thing is to get into a rhythm and routine of writing, morning pages are a great help in this regard, but making writing a habit is crucial. The other thing is not to beat yourself up when you've only written 100 words that day, or missed a couple of days. Any momentum is forward momentum and feeling guilty about your writing only stands in the way of you finishing your novel.

~ CK MacLeod ~

www.techtoolsforwriters.com

(1) Have a system. In order to write a quality book, it helps to know what steps are essential to producing that quality. In Idea to Ebook: How to Write a Quality Book Fast, I list the writing and publishing steps that authors can follow in order

to produce a quality read. I also suggest ways to make those steps efficient. Your time is valuable, and if there's another way to create great book in less time, I want to know about it!

(2) You have many options for formatting an ebook, from DIY to hire. The most cost-effective way is to begin with the tool you have. What tool are you using to write your book? Can you use that tool to also format your book? Find out everything you can about the tool you already have.

(3) I'm not a marketing expert by any stretch – at least not yet. But I have picked up two tips that can't hurt: Learn to summarize your book in one compelling sentence. People's attention spans are short. Practice on Twitter.

Also, consider asking people from your social media networks to review your book. Send them a free review copy and ask them to be transparent about that when they post their review. I belong to a professional editing organization and it only just occurred to me that I can ask my colleagues to review my book!

(4) No one writes like you do. Every author has a voice and a style that's unique and a perspective on a topic that is theirs alone. Exercise your writing muscles. Read, read, read, and write, write, write. Cultivate that writing voice. It's like a thumbprint – there are no two alike.

FREE POSTER

I put up some of the quotes in this book on Twitter: the one that resonated the most seems to be the section image for "Publish" by Margaret Atwood ("Publishing a book is like stuffing a note into a bottle…"). It got retweeted about 160 times in 24 hours. So I'm going to print that up as a poster and mail it to anybody who reviews this book before August 30th. If you want one, just email me a copy of the review you posted and your shipping address, (I promise you won't get any junk mail, I won't even keep a record of your details.) Put "Free Poster" in the subject line to make sure I see it.

My email: derekmurphy@creativindie.com

THANKS

Thanks again for purchasing this book; I hope you learned at least a little something useful – if you didn't, I hope the free resources on www.diybookformats.com or www.diybookcovers.com will save you a lot of time and money.

On my blog "Creativindie" I help authors and artists produce and sell their best work, and become financially and creatively independent. One of the fun things I've been doing recently is giving away my TimeShare weeks for authors to use as a "Writer's Vacation." I give away a couple a year, so you may want to join my email list or my Facebook page to stay in the loop.

Feel free to contact me with publishing questions. Although I'm also experimenting with writing and publishing, I've had a lot of experience and am starting to see some huge gains. I hope that together, we can all become fabulously wealthy self-published authors and buy retirement houses in exotic settings, and meet up for martinis and foot massages.

ABOUT THE AUTHOR

 DEREK MURPHY has been a book cover designer, writing coach and publishing consultant for almost a decade, working behind the scenes with hundreds of indie and self-publishing authors to make their books more successful. He currently teaches authors and artists how to turn their passions into full-time businesses, make a bigger impact, and blaze a luminous trail of creative independence.

Besides publishing, Derek is an avid traveller with an interest in history and literature. He's lived in Argentina, Malta and Taiwan, and traveled extensively through dozens of countries. He's been a national representative for Amnesty International, and is close to finishing a PHD in Philosophy and Comparative Literature.

Connect with Derek or Twitter or Facebook
Twitter: @creativindie
Facebook: @creativindie
Email: derekmurphy@creativindie.com